COLOSSIANS
AND PHILEMON

WORD and SPIRIT COMMENTARY ON THE NEW TESTAMENT

SERIES EDITORS

Craig S. Keener, Asbury Theological Seminary
Holly Beers, Westmont College

ADVISORY BOARD

Gordon D. Fee†, Regent College
J. Ayodeji Adewuya, Pentecostal Theological Seminary
Lisa Marie Bowens, Princeton Theological Seminary
Jacob Cherian, Centre for Global Leadership Development
Robert Menzies, Asia Pacific Theological Seminary

VOLUMES NOW AVAILABLE

Romans   Sam Storms
2 Corinthians   Ben Witherington III
Colossians and Philemon   Holly Beers

COLOSSIANS
AND PHILEMON

Holly Beers

ℬ

Baker Academic

a division of Baker Publishing Group

Grand Rapids, Michigan

Published by Baker Academic
a division of Baker Publishing Group
Grand Rapids, Michigan
BakerAcademic.com

Printed in the United States of America

Library of Congress Cataloging-in-Publication Data
Names: Beers, Holly, author.
Title: Colossians and Philemon / Holly Beers.
Description: Grand Rapids, Michigan : Baker Academic, a division of Baker Publishing Group, 2025. | Series: Word and spirit commentary on the New Testament | Includes bibliographical references and index.
Identifiers: LCCN 2024024334 | ISBN 9781540963864 (paperback) | ISBN 9781540968623 (casebound) | ISBN 9781493449255 (ebook) | ISBN 9781493449262 (pdf)
Subjects: LCSH: Bible. Colossians—Commentaries. | Bible. Philemon—Commentaries.
Classification: LCC BS2715.53 .B44 2025 | DDC 227/.707—dc23/eng/20240609
LC record available at https://lccn.loc.gov/2024024334

Baker Publishing Group publications use paper produced from sustainable forestry practices and post-consumer waste whenever possible.

25 26 27 28 29 30 31   7 6 5 4 3 2 1

Contents

Series Preface

In the foreword to Roger Stronstad's 1984 volume *The Charismatic Theology of St. Luke*, Clark H. Pinnock wrote, "The young Pentecostal scholars are coming!"[1] That was a generation ago, and now the pentecostal scholars are here, many of them having grown up alongside the explosive global growth of charismatic and pentecostal traditions. Such growth has been well documented,[2] with the number of adherents estimated at more than half a billion. In many places, Bible teaching has not been able to keep pace with this growth. Because of this reality, there is a clear need for a balanced commentary series aimed at Christians who identify as Spirit-filled, including renewalists, charismatics, and pentecostals, as well as others who want to learn more from this sphere of the church.

Because so many within these traditions often use wider evangelical literature, this series is sensitive to those intellectual and academic standards. However, others mistrust what they see as "purely intellectual" approaches, and they will find that this series also focuses on how the same Spirit who inspired the text speaks and works today. In this way the series offers a conversation for the church rather than operating primarily as a forum for discussion among scholars.

The commentary proper in each volume engages the biblical text both in its ancient setting and with regard to its message for Spirit-filled Christians

1. Clark H. Pinnock, foreword to *The Charismatic Theology of St. Luke*, by Roger Stronstad (Peabody, MA: Hendrickson, 1984), vii.
2. For example, Peter L. Berger, "Four Faces of Global Culture," in *Globalization and the Challenges of a New Century: A Reader*, ed. Patrick O'Meara, Howard D. Mehlinger, and Matthew Krain (Bloomington: Indiana University Press, 2000), 425; Robert Bruce Mullin, *A Short World History of Christianity* (Louisville: Westminster John Knox, 2008), 211 (compare 276); Mark A. Noll, *The New Shape of World Christianity: How American Experience Reflects Global Faith* (Downers Grove, IL: IVP Academic, 2009), 32.

today. The commentaries often integrate exegesis and application, as readers in charismatic and pentecostal traditions tend to move naturally between these categories rather than separating them. In other words, such readers traditionally blend the ancient and modern horizons so as to read themselves within the continuing narrative of salvation history—that is, as part of the ongoing biblical story (not part of ancient culture but as theologically/spiritually/eschatologically part of God's same church).

As part of the blending of horizons, distinctive interests for Spirit-filled audiences are addressed when relevant. These include—but are not limited to—the reality of the new birth, healing and other miracles, spiritual gifts, hearing God's voice, the working of the Spirit in daily life, spiritual warfare, and so on. Not all biblical texts, and thus not all exposition, focuses on these points alone, and our authors do not artificially impose these topics on passages that do not naturally address them. In other words, our authors observe how God works in the biblical texts and how Christians can expect God to be working today, even if in new or culturally surprising ways.

However, each author also writes from within a charismatic, renewalist, or pentecostal context across the broad spectrum of the Spirit-focused tradition, and the authors often refer to such spaces in their writing. The range of voices includes denominational Pentecostals, Reformed charismatics, charismatic Methodists, and others. They also reflect a range of cultures, including Spirit-filled voices from multiple continents.

The authors "preach" their way through the texts, hosting a conversation both as trusted insiders for their own home traditions and as hospitable guides for others who wish to listen again alongside the ancient audiences for the Spirit's voice in our time and contexts. The commentaries are written with other distinctives of the tradition(s), including the incorporation of testimony and sidebars that feature connections to pentecostal/charismatic/revival history, teaching, and practice.

Other sidebars focus on biblical background and lengthier points of application. The series has adopted the NIV as the default text, as it is widely used in contexts that identify as Spirit-filled. However, our authors will often reference other translations, including their own. Quoted biblical texts from the passage under discussion will be highlighted in bold. Greek words are transliterated.

We offer this series to the church, and we pray that it testifies to the creative work and restorative goodness of the triune God.

Holly Beers, Westmont College
Craig S. Keener, Asbury Theological Seminary

Acknowledgments

For Bryan Dyer at Baker Academic, who first joined me in dreaming about the possibility of this series.

For Craig Keener, my big brother in Christ, for being the kind of gracious senior scholar that I hope to be someday.

For the students in my course on Colossians and Philemon at Westmont College in the fall of 2022, who read the entire draft of this volume, engaging it with curiosity and offering insightful feedback: Halle Booher, Colin Brown, Macy Kate Cholometes, Nik Day, Caroline Eaton, Anika J. Erlenborn, Faith German, Emma Hester, Madden Hundley, Ava Hunt, Caleb Liebengood, Caleb Marll, Peyton Lindman Marshall, Emma Mitchell, Lindsay Jewel Morales, Miles Ozorio, Theo Patterson, Cade Roth, Maddy Simonsen, Callie K. Smith, Gabie Smith, Elyse Wagner, and Ben Work.

And for my kids, who are part of my daily testimonies (including some in this book), and my husband, Max, with whom I live a rhythmic mutuality as we teach and admonish each other (Col. 3:16).

Abbreviations

Old Testament

Gen.	Genesis	2 Chron.	2 Chronicles	Dan.	Daniel
Exod.	Exodus	Ezra	Ezra	Hosea	Hosea
Lev.	Leviticus	Neh.	Nehemiah	Joel	Joel
Num.	Numbers	Esther	Esther	Amos	Amos
Deut.	Deuteronomy	Job	Job	Obad.	Obadiah
Josh.	Joshua	Ps(s).	Psalm(s)	Jon.	Jonah
Judg.	Judges	Prov.	Proverbs	Mic.	Micah
Ruth	Ruth	Eccles.	Ecclesiastes	Nah.	Nahum
1 Sam.	1 Samuel	Song	Song of Songs	Hab.	Habakkuk
2 Sam.	2 Samuel	Isa.	Isaiah	Zeph.	Zephaniah
1 Kings	1 Kings	Jer.	Jeremiah	Hag.	Haggai
2 Kings	2 Kings	Lam.	Lamentations	Zech.	Zechariah
1 Chron.	1 Chronicles	Ezek.	Ezekiel	Mal.	Malachi

New Testament

Matt.	Matthew	Eph.	Ephesians	Heb.	Hebrews
Mark	Mark	Phil.	Philippians	James	James
Luke	Luke	Col.	Colossians	1 Pet.	1 Peter
John	John	1 Thess.	1 Thessalonians	2 Pet.	2 Peter
Acts	Acts	2 Thess.	2 Thessalonians	1 John	1 John
Rom.	Romans	1 Tim.	1 Timothy	2 John	2 John
1 Cor.	1 Corinthians	2 Tim.	2 Timothy	3 John	3 John
2 Cor.	2 Corinthians	Titus	Titus	Jude	Jude
Gal.	Galatians	Philem.	Philemon	Rev.	Revelation

Modern Versions

KJV	King James Version
NIV	New International Version
NRSV	New Revised Standard Version

General

AT	author's translation
ca.	circa
s.v.	*sub verbo*, under the word
//	parallel text(s)

Introduction

Authorship

Church tradition has always affirmed that the apostle Paul is the author of Colossians and Philemon, and even today Paul is universally viewed as the author of Philemon. Some scholars, however, have raised doubts about the authorship of Colossians, giving as reasons the different style (in Greek), vocabulary, and theology when compared to letters such as Romans, 1 Corinthians, and Galatians. For example, some of Paul's favorite vocabulary terms, such as "law," are missing from Colossians. On the other hand, there are clear similarities between Colossians and Ephesians (for example, the language about "psalms, hymns, and songs from the Spirit" in Col. 3:16 // Eph. 3:19; the household code in Col. 3:18–4:1 // Eph. 5:21–6:9; the "mystery" [*mystērion*] in Col. 1:26–27; 2:2; 4:3 // Eph. 1:9; 3:3–4, 9; 5:32; 6:19), but some scholars also doubt whether Paul wrote Ephesians. Many insist that if Paul did not write these letters, the author was in the "Pauline circle" and likely knew Paul and/or the content of his other letters well.

Many scholars today do affirm Pauline authorship of both Colossians and Philemon, insisting that questions of style, vocabulary, and content should be evaluated with at least two factors in mind: scribes and context. First, it was typical in the ancient Mediterranean region, even for persons who could read and write, to use a scribe (also called an amanuensis) to write letters. Paul's letters contain references to scribes who helped with them, sometimes directly (in Rom. 16:22 Tertius says that he "wrote down this letter") and sometimes indirectly (Timothy is listed as a coauthor in both Col. 1:1 and Philem. 1, which could indicate his role as scribe).[1] Because scribes often were given permission to shape

---

1. Timothy is not listed as a coauthor in Ephesians.

letters rather than just copy what was dictated, it makes sense that, for Colossians, Timothy would have participated in the content, choice of vocabulary, and style.

Second, the context matters, as Paul is writing Colossians to a group of Christians in a specific place. Good communicators tailor their messages to different groups; they do not say the exact same thing in the same way every time. Paul, as a master contextualizer, would have had the wisdom and experience to shape the Letter to the Colossians (with Timothy's help, of course) in ways that made sense for people living in Colossae. It is also worth noting that Paul writes different letters at different points in his ministry, which means that the way in which he communicates ideas may have shifted a bit, depending on his own growth and exposure to new ideas. All of this means that Paul should still be seen as the author of Colossians. In fact, no one in the early church doubted the authorship of this letter.

Historical Context

Colossians and Philemon among the Prison Epistles

There are four New Testament epistles traditionally referred to as the Prison Epistles because they indicate that Paul was in prison while writing them. Prisons in the ancient Mediterranean world typically were not buildings (except in cases of house arrest [see Acts 28:30]) but rather were holes in the ground or caves that had been converted for such use. Prisoners were not often given food, water, or other supplies; they relied on family and friends for these necessities (see Matt. 25:36, 39). These sites also were used mainly as temporary holding places for prisoners awaiting official trial or punishment; they were not used as punishment in and of themselves (unlike their use in many contexts today). Prisons often were dark, smelly, and dangerous, as assault was common.

It is in such a place that Paul wrote both Colossians and Philemon (Col. 4:3–4, 18; Philem. 1, 9, 23); they are two of the four Prison Epistles, alongside Ephesians and Philippians (Eph. 3:1; 4:1; Phil. 1:12–14). Because Paul was in prison multiple times (2 Cor. 6:4–5; 11:23–27), there are questions about the location and timing for each of these letters. The traditional Christian view has been that all four were written during Paul's imprisonment in Rome in the early AD 60s, although other locations and dates have also been suggested, including Caesarea (Acts 23:33–26:32) and Ephesus (see 2 Cor. 11:23, written before the other imprisonments; also Acts 20:16; 1 Cor. 15:32; 2 Cor. 1:8). This could push the date of writing for the letters earlier to the mid-to-early AD 50s.

Colossians and Philemon are often grouped and read together, at least partly because they address people who lived in the same city, Colossae. The city of

Colossae

Colossae is located in modern Türkiye, in the province called Asia Minor during the time of the New Testament. It appears to have been a fairly unremarkable ancient city in the first century AD, though its location in the fertile Lycus Valley was advantageous. Neighboring cities such as Laodicea and Hierapolis, along with Ephesus, eclipsed it in importance. At this point we have only historical descriptions as a basis for comparison, as the city of Colossae has not yet been excavated. The good news is that the archaeological work is scheduled to begin soon.

There was a significant earthquake in AD 60 in Colossae, and scholars thought for years that the city was destroyed and not rebuilt. If so, this would have affected the dating of the letters, as it would have given a firm end date. However, new evidence demonstrates that Colossae likely was restored.[2] The city had a substantial Jewish population, though the church addressed in the Letter to the Colossians appears to be primarily gentile/non-Jewish and uncircumcised (Col. 2:11, 13).

Philemon, the one addressed in the Letter to Philemon, is the master/owner of Onesimus, a slave (Philem. 16). In the letter, Paul appears to have been close friends with Philemon. The question is, then, whether the two letters were written at separate times or the same time. If the same time, they would have been sent together to Colossae. Is the slave Onesimus (if it is in fact the same Onesimus as in Philem. 10), along with Tychicus, bringing both letters (Col. 4:7–9), one of which tells slaves to obey their masters (Col. 3:22)—though stringent expectations are placed on masters as well with the command "provide your slaves with what is right and fair" (4:1)—while the other asks for Philemon to receive Onesimus as a brother *rather than* as a slave (Philem. 16)?

2. Cadwallader, "Colossae."

If Paul did indeed write Colossians, and did so before writing Philemon, then Onesimus would have carried the Letter to the Colossians first. Afterward Onesimus engages in some kind of problem or dispute with his master, Philemon (Philem. 11, 18). It is at that point that Paul pushes Philemon to respond differently to his slave, at least in terms of specific, personal instructions. If Philemon was written before Colossians, then Paul initially exhorted Philemon to welcome his slave Onesimus as a brother but then later reframed his comments regarding slavery in order to address a broader church—one that he did not know well and did not plant (Col. 1:7 [see comments there])—as his primary audience.[3]

My own view is that the exact dating and order of Colossians and Philemon do not matter all that much, as the specific recipients shape the argument in each letter. As just stated, Paul did not seem to know most people in the Colossian church very well, with a few exceptions. Philemon, whom Paul could have met in the neighboring city of Ephesus (where Paul did spend a lot of time [Acts 19:1, 8, 10, 21–22]), clearly was a close friend of Paul. In the context of that relationship Paul is able to speak very directly and even assertively regarding the situation with the slave Onesimus.

Primary Historical Issue: Slavery in the Ancient Mediterranean World

As already mentioned, slavery is a key historical issue for understanding both Colossians and Philemon. My primary context is the United States, which has its own history of slavery, but it is important to note that histories of slavery have both similarities and differences. The primary difference between the United States and the ancient Mediterranean world is that in the former slavery was racialized and based primarily on skin color, while in the latter it was not.

In Paul's context people became enslaved in a variety of ways. One was conquest, whereby one group conquered another and took slaves from their population. Another was debt, as people could sell themselves into slavery. This kind of slavery often was temporary, lasting until the debt was paid. Some people became slaves because they were kidnapped, including by pirates. Some children were born to slaves (and became slaves themselves), but some unwanted children also became slaves. Such children were abandoned, and slavers picked them up and raised them until they were old enough to be sold as slaves. Often the reason for abandonment was economic: children were more mouths to feed, which was challenging in a context where most people were simply trying to

---

3. Also, Paul stresses at the end of Philemon (v. 22) that he hopes to visit soon, which could indicate that this letter was written first. Paul seems to find a visit likely, whereas in Colossians a visit is not mentioned.

survive. Sometimes the reason was gendered, as boys often were preferred to girls. Sometimes disability was the reason. It was actually fairly common in the ancient Mediterranean world for *non-Jews* to kill or abandon unwanted infants; sometimes in major cities there were publicly known locations where people could leave children. Importantly, Jews and Christians were (in)famous in that world for opposing the practice of infanticide and child abandonment; their commitment to God's value on human life and humans as God's image bearers provided a different lens for viewing children.

In terms of similarities between slavery in the ancient Mediterranean world and in the United States prior to abolition,[4] the main connection is that the institution of slavery was simply an everyday part of both contexts; it was a cultural norm in that many people seem to have assumed that it was simply how the world worked. In the Roman Empire the economy was built on it; that is true of other economies throughout history as well, of course.

In terms of percentage of population, perhaps 10–15 percent were enslaved in the outer edges of the Roman Empire and up to 30 percent in/near Rome itself. Everyone would have known a slave (or been enslaved themselves); there certainly were slaves in the church in Colossae, as Paul talks to them in Colossians (Col. 3:22–25 [see extended comments there]) and highlights the slave Onesimus in Philemon (vv. 10, 16). The distinction between slave and free was one of the most obvious in their context. People were separated into those who owned their own agency, labor, and sexuality, and those who did not because they were owned by someone else. This is another point of connection between ancient Mediterranean slavery and more recent versions, including in the United States. Many slaves (including male and female, young and old) were sexually abused by (male and female) masters, though both cultures often did not consider that to be abuse. Such sexual unions often produced offspring, and while slaves were not legally allowed to marry, many entered into informal unions with other enslaved people.[5]

In the Roman Empire some texts expressed opposition to extremely harsh treatment of slaves, but most ancient sources were not worried about what we (not they) would call abuse. Even the sources that opposed harsh treatment often gave as the reason protection of property ("property" as both the slaves themselves and the work that obedient slaves did to earn better profits for their

---

4. In the 1700s, most took slavery for granted in the United States, though not everyone did so, especially some Christians (including some Anglicans, Quakers, Methodists, and evangelicals). Their Christian conviction was the main reason slavery came to be seen as problematic in the United States.

5. For discussion of the complex relationships that enslaved people would have managed, see MacDonald, *Power of Children*.

masters) rather than the dignity and personhood of the slave. The most common cultural view was that slaves were inferior to free people both morally and intellectually.[6]

Slaves worked in every area imaginable, from acting as wet nurses and nannies, to agricultural laboring, to teaching, to managing. Some slaves owned other slaves, which indicates that there was stratification even within the slave population. Some slaves were relatively well educated (by or with the approval of their masters), whereas some were not. Sometimes enslaved people could find their freedom; masters sometimes manumitted slaves, though often there was still a cultural expectation that the former slave (now freedperson) would remain loyal and connected socially to their former master. The freedperson would then function as a client who owed honor (in the form of public praise or other public offerings) to the former master as the patron. Sometimes enslaved people could purchase their freedom.

Slavery in Colossians and Philemon

As the Letters to the Colossians and to Philemon make clear, enslaved people were part of the early church. The household code in Col. 3:18–4:1 contains instructions to slaves and masters (see detailed commentary there), and the Letter to Philemon discusses the enslaved man Onesimus (vv. 10, 16). The common view regarding Onesimus is that he was a runaway slave,[7] but that is only one of the options. The situation is unclear because the letter itself does not explain the circumstances; Paul did not need to do so, of course, as he and Philemon and Onesimus all knew what had transpired.

If Onesimus was indeed a runaway slave, then he was in danger, both from the authorities (including slave catchers) and from his master if he returned. Public notices for runaway slaves often were posted; sometimes slaves were tattooed as evidence of ownership if they had run away and were recaptured. Severe punishments for disobedient slaves were expected and legal, though the possibility existed that a slave could seek legal protection from an overly harsh master. This matters because if Paul is sending a runaway Onesimus back to a potentially angry and shamed Philemon (Philem. 10–12, 18), Onesimus is being exposed to potential abuse or death. Many readers of the Bible have wondered

---

6. See Thompson, *Colossians and Philemon*, 220–21, including her sources.

7. This understanding goes back to the church father John Chrysostom, in the fourth century AD, in his *Homiliae in epistulam ad Philemonem*. Some scholars have doubted this option because it does not explain how Onesimus would have met Paul if Paul was in prison (and Onesimus was not). The answer might be as simple as a divine appointment, with Onesimus meeting or seeing a friend in the marketplace who was a Christian and knew Paul. The letter does not explain this background information; perhaps everyone already knew it.

about the justice of such an act. Should Paul have returned Onesimus if it endangered him, especially when slavery itself is unjust? This is a fair question in our contexts today, though Paul's context needs to be taken seriously as well. For example, there were penalties for harboring runaway slaves, so in this scenario Paul was also putting himself at risk.[8]

A second option is that Onesimus may not have been a runaway but instead have had some kind of conflict with his master, Philemon. Perhaps Onesimus was a manager in Philemon's business and made a poor financial decision. In this scenario Onesimus would have gone intentionally to find Paul and ask for his help in mediating the situation with Philemon; during the course of this interaction Onesimus became a Christian (Philem. 10). In this case Onesimus might not be in terrible physical danger if/when he returns to Philemon, and Paul's support of him (as evidenced through the Letter to Philemon) would encourage a positive reception. A related option is that Philemon sent Onesimus to help Paul in prison,[9] and Onesimus became a Christian while there. In the letter Paul is encouraging Philemon to receive Onesimus appropriately on his return and then send him back to help Paul (v. 11). This makes the question of debt a hypothetical rather than actual one (v. 18).

Two more options should be mentioned, though most scholars have not found these views to be persuasive. One is that the man Archippus—not Philemon—is the owner of Onesimus. Archippus is named along with Philemon and Apphia in the letter (Philem. 1–2), and in Colossians the church is instructed, "Tell Archippus: 'See to it that you complete the ministry you have received in the Lord'" (Col. 4:17 [see comments there]). This "ministry" could be the welcome (and possibly even the manumission) of Onesimus if Onesimus is his slave.[10] The second minority view is that Philemon and Onesimus are in fact (blood) brothers involved in a dispute that is serious enough for one to be labeled a "slave" (Philem. 16); Paul is arguing in the letter for a full reconciliation between these brothers.[11]

My own view is that the most important historical issue is not whether Onesimus was a runaway slave but rather the way in which Paul advocates for

---

8. There is also a question about how this text from Deuteronomy fits: "Slaves who have escaped to you from their owners shall not be given back to them. They shall reside with you, in your midst, in any place they choose in any one of your towns, wherever they please; you shall not oppress them" (Deut. 23:15–16 NRSV). This instruction is given to Israel, so the question is how it applies in a situation involving the church, where the boundaries between Israelites (like Paul) and non-Israelites (as apparently Philemon and Onesimus both were) have changed. For discussion, see Beale, *Colossians and Philemon*, 416.

9. Eric Barreto takes this view ("Philemon," 615).

10. This view was made famous by Knox, *Philemon*.

11. See Callahan, "Paul's Epistle to Philemon."

someone who cannot return the favor. In a world where slavery is the status quo, both culturally and legally, how does a free person use their social capital for an enslaved person? A related question is whether Paul's advocacy was successful or not; this depends at least partly on the order in which we think the letters were written. If Philemon is first, is Onesimus's later arrival with the other letter (Col. 4:9) proof that Philemon did what Paul had asked? Also, the church father Ignatius, who died in the second century AD, mentions a man named Onesimus as the bishop of Ephesus.[12] If this is the same man, it indicates that Philemon was faithful in his response and even (apparently) manumitted his slave, who later became a leader in the church.

The church over the centuries has read the slavery texts in Colossians and Philemon in a variety of ways.[13] In the early church the Letter to Philemon especially did not receive a great deal of attention; it was viewed as mundane and even unspiritual. Later, in contexts like the United States, these slavery texts were used by both pro- and antislavery advocates to argue for their positions,[14] though pro-slavery authors often read biblical texts out of context (and appealed to secular sources like the Constitution), whereas antislavery authors discussed the ancient Mediterranean culture and pointed to the liberating trajectory of the Bible.[15] For example, if we read the 1850 Fugitive Slave Act, passed by the US Congress, we can hear the language that was shaped by Philemon, as it affirms that escaped slaves should be returned to their masters. Today scholars are reading Philemon and the slavery passage in Colossians more carefully than ever, contextualizing them with the best of what we know about ancient Mediterranean slavery and Paul's attempts to disciple people in the gospel.

Genre, Structure, Themes

The genre of both Colossians and Philemon is letter or epistle. There was a commonly accepted letter format in ancient Mediterranean culture that is largely followed by Paul, including in Colossians and Philemon. First, there are the introductory matters, which include the identification of the author(s) and audience, a greeting (typically Paul offers grace and peace), and a thanksgiving (to God and for the audience). Then the body of the letter follows; here it is important to pay attention to the development of Paul's argument. What is he

12. See Ignatius, *To the Ephesians*.

13. For a detailed and helpful summary of how the Letter to Philemon has been understood and used, see Williams, "'No Longer as a Slave.'"

14. For many examples, see Bowens, *African American Readings*.

15. For details, see Keener and Usry, *Defending Black Faith*; Usry and Keener, *Black Man's Religion*.

saying and why? What is the issue or problem at hand, and how is Paul addressing it? Finally, Paul concludes with personal news, greetings, and a brief farewell that often functions as a benediction.

Colossians

Many have identified the heart of the Letter to the Colossians in the following verses: "So then, just as you received Christ Jesus as Lord, continue to live your lives in him, rooted and built up in him, strengthened in the faith as you were taught, and overflowing with thankfulness" (Col. 2:6–7). Whether or not we see this as the heart of the letter, it is true that these verses contain key themes, including the focus on Christ, the need to stay rooted in him, and the practice of thankfulness.

The need to stay rooted is connected to the problem of false teaching and practices, as most of Col. 2 makes clear. Nowhere does Paul give a comprehensive description of who the false teachers are and exactly what they are teaching, but there are clues in the letter. There are elements that are Jewish in origin (as the comment about Sabbath in 2:16 makes clear), but other aspects could just as easily be non-Jewish. For example, some gentiles also stressed fasting practices in various religious settings (2:21–23). The church as a whole appears to be predominantly gentile, in fact (see 2:11, 13, and note the references to circumcision).

In other words, there appears to be a syncretism at work in the church that is combining various elements. We do not know of any overall system or religion that exactly matches this description, but that may be due to the fact that the city of Colossae has not yet been excavated. In light of the Jewish elements, we need to be careful here not to be anti-Semitic. Paul is a Jew, just like Jesus, and any critique of Jewish elements does not mean that he is excluding or demeaning his entire ethnic group. Rather, his argument is that Christ offers fullness and the true reality (2:9–10, 17), which means that Jesus ushers in the final goal and purpose for the world. This good news or gospel, then, is distinctly Jewish, as Paul argues throughout his letters.

The main themes in Colossians all respond to the false teaching by reinforcing this Jesus-shaped hope, with a primary theme being Christ's cosmic fullness or even supremacy, in both creation and the renewal of creation (see especially 1:15–20, a highly developed Christology). This includes Christ's defeat of the powers (2:15), which should shape the way that Christians live (3:1–4:6). The emphasis on Christian behavior and lifestyle is important here because it shows that the beauty of Christ's work is already accomplished in one sense (this is called "realized eschatology"), but it is still awaiting final fulfillment in another sense (as it needs to be lived, not just assented to). Many scholars have argued that Colossians teaches primarily a realized eschatology, and this may be true in the first half of the letter. However, the second half demonstrates that God's restorative project for the world—what Paul calls the gospel—is inaugurated but not yet completely finished.

Philemon

The primary theme of Philemon is also connected to the gospel as God's restorative project for all of creation. Here, however, that project is filtered through the relationships between Paul, a master named Philemon, and his slave Onesimus. Here God's plan to (re)create a human family through Jesus—where all are brothers and sisters (Philem. 16)—must not simply be accepted intellectually but be embodied. The cost of discipleship was high for an ancient Christian slave owner, and the cost is high for Paul as well, as he risks his friendship with Philemon in order to urge him to participate more fully in the kingdom of God through the way that he welcomes and treats Onesimus.

Narrative and Theological Relationship to Paul's Letters and the Entire Bible, for Ancient Colossians and for Us Today

The Letters to the Colossians and to Philemon contribute powerfully to a broader understanding of the Bible. Like the rest of Paul's letters, they rely on an understanding of the Old Testament and how Israel fits into God's plan to restore creation,[16] as they see Jesus Christ as the fulfillment of this plan. Jesus is thus the hinge of God's kingdom reality. In Colossians the focus is cosmic (as in Ephesians, a sister letter to Colossians that aligns in structure and content); in Philemon the focus is on the relationships between three individuals. More specifically, in both letters Paul does what he always does: discipleship. His task in this way is consistent, as again and again he works with real people in real life, persuading them to adopt a posture toward *the gospel as truly good news* that reshapes how they live their lives. These early Christians are in different places in their walks of faith, which is at least partly why Paul's directions to them are not identical. The instructions to slaves and masters in Colossians are different than what Paul encourages the master Philemon to do with his slave Onesimus (Col. 3:22–4:1; Philem. 16), but the goal is the same: move them forward, toward greater confidence and maturity, in Jesus.

---

16. This is true even if there are few direct references to the Old Testament in these letters. Subtle references do not necessarily indicate a lack of knowledge; rather, they can indicate a depth of knowledge, as an allusion will be caught by those who know the material well.

And what is our posture toward the gospel? Are we living as if God's restorative plan, with Jesus at the center of it, is truly good news? Is it reshaping our lives, our discipleship? Put differently: Are we hearing what the Spirit is saying to us through the text? Are we able to make the connection between what the Spirit said to Paul's audience and what that means for us today? Are we honoring the reality that the Spirit inspired Paul to speak to these ancient people first, and that the Spirit's message to us must be aligned with that ancient truth? All biblical books are shaped by their first contexts, of course. We are not the first of God's people, but we can and should see ourselves in the stories of discipleship that have preceded us in our sacred texts. The Spirit wants us to hear well so that we can walk forward, toward greater confidence and maturity, in Jesus.

Outline

Colossians

1. Greeting the Colossians (1:1–2)
2. Thanksgiving to God and praise for the Colossians (1:3–8)
3. Casting the vision for the reality of what is true in Christ (1:9–3:4)
   A. Rescue and inheritance through Christ (1:9–14)
   B. Christ as creator and redeemer of creation (1:15–23)
   C. The mystery of Christ revealed to us (1:24–2:7)
   D. Fullness in Christ as a challenge to idolatry (2:8–3:4)
4. Embodying the reality of what is true in Christ (3:5–4:6)
   A. Resisting vices and embodying virtues (3:5–17)
   B. Embodying Christ in the household (3:18–4:1)
   C. Embodying Christ in the world (4:2–6)
5. Final greetings and blessing (4:7–18)

Philemon

1. Greeting Philemon and the church (vv. 1–3)
2. Thanksgiving to God and praise for Philemon (vv. 4–7)
3. Paul's appeal for Onesimus (vv. 8–22)
4. Final greetings and blessing (vv. 23–25)

Recommended Resources

Barreto, Eric D. "Philemon." In *The Fortress Commentary on the Bible: The New Testament*, edited by Margaret Aymer, Cynthia Briggs Kittredge, and David A. Sánchez, 613–20. Minneapolis: Fortress, 2014.

Dunn, James D. G. *The Epistles to the Colossians and to Philemon: A Commentary on the Greek Text*. New International Greek Testament Commentary. Grand Rapids: Eerdmans, 1996.

Keesmaat, Sylvia C. "Colossians." In *The Fortress Commentary on the Bible: The New Testament*, edited by Margaret Aymer, Cynthia Briggs Kittredge, and David A. Sánchez, 557–72. Minneapolis: Fortress, 2014.

Lewis, Lloyd A. "Colossians." In *True to Our Native Land: An African American New Testament Commentary*, edited by Brian K. Blount, 380–88. Minneapolis: Fortress, 2007.

———. "Philemon." In *True to Our Native Land: An African American New Testament Commentary*, edited by Brian K. Blount, 437–43. Minneapolis: Fortress, 2007.

Lyons, George, Robert W. Smith, and Kara Lyons-Pardue. *Ephesians, Colossians, Philemon: A Commentary in the Wesleyan Tradition*. New Beacon Bible Commentary. Boston: Beacon Hill, 2019.

MacDonald, Margaret Y. *Colossians and Ephesians*. Sacra Pagina 17. Collegeville, MN: Liturgical Press, 2000.

McKnight, Scot. *The Letter to Philemon*. New International Commentary on the New Testament. Grand Rapids: Eerdmans, 2017.

———. *The Letter to the Colossians*. New International Commentary on the New Testament. Grand Rapids: Eerdmans, 2018.

Pao, David. *Colossians and Philemon*. Zondervan Exegetical Commentary on the New Testament. Grand Rapids: Zondervan, 2012.

Sumney, Jerry L. *Colossians: A Commentary*. New Testament Library. Louisville: Westminster John Knox, 2008.

Thompson, Marianne Meye. *Colossians and Philemon*. Two Horizons New Testament Commentary. Grand Rapids: Eerdmans, 2005.

Wintle, Bruce, and Bruce Nicholls. *Colossians and Philemon: A Pastoral and Contextual Commentary*. Asia Bible Commentary. Carlisle: Langham Global Library, 2019.

Wright, N. T. *Colossians and Philemon: An Introduction and Commentary*. Tyndale New Testament Commentaries 12. Downers Grove, IL: IVP Academic, 2008.

Colossians

Greeting the Colossians

Colossians 1:1 begins in a manner typical of ancient Mediterranean letters, including Paul's own. Paul mentions himself as author, and then he includes his coworker Timothy as a dual author, which could indicate that Timothy was the secretary, having written the letter down, though he may also have contributed to some of the content. Timothy is listed as a coauthor with Paul elsewhere (2 Cor. 1:1 [see also v. 19]; Phil. 1:1 [see also 2:19]; 1 Thess. 1:1; 2 Thess. 1:1; Philem. 1), and beyond his role as author, Timothy is clearly a key coworker of Paul (Rom. 16:21; 1 Thess. 3:2 [see also v. 6]; 1 Tim. 1:2; 2 Tim. 1:2), and he appears in numerous places in New Testament texts, often alongside others who labor for the gospel.[1] Acts describes Paul's first encounter with Timothy when Timothy joins the Jesus-movement (16:1–3), and Timothy remains a close part of Paul's circle throughout the New Testament.

These many references illustrate a key point regarding Paul's life and ministry that remains relevant today: he is not a lone ranger. His work as apostle and missionary is not a solo task but rather is undertaken within a team framework. The few instances where Paul is alone, such as in Acts 17 in Athens, are temporary and exceptions (due to persecution). The dangers of solo leadership today are well known, especially the lack of accountability and support, and Paul's example reminds us that even authors of New Testament books understood that God values communal leadership. This is consistent with the rest of the New Testament, which sees even local, permanent church leadership as group-oriented

1. See Acts 16:1; 17:14–15; 18:5; 19:22; 20:4; 1 Cor. 4:17; 16:10; 1 Tim. 1:2, 18; 6:20; 2 Tim. 1:2; Heb. 13:23.

rather than singular.[2] The example often cited from 1–2 Timothy, where Timothy himself is understood by many to be the singular leader of the church, overlooks the way in which Paul describes Timothy's time in Ephesus as temporary. It is the local elders who will remain in Ephesus long after Timothy has departed (1 Tim. 1:3; 2 Tim. 4:9). The same is true for Titus (Titus 1:5; 3:12). This fits well with the broader picture of mutuality and service among followers of Jesus in the New Testament, who are to teach and warn one another (Col. 3:16) and address questions and issues in their local assembly together, as a group (for example, 1 Cor. 5:4–5; 11:17–14:40).

All of this raises questions for the ways in which many Christian leaders today operate. Even if there is a board of elders or leadership team in place, in reality one leader often dominates or greatly underutilizes the team that God has put in place around them. From a cultural perspective it may make sense, as the president or CEO of a business may operate similarly, but the people of God are not (primarily) a business when they gather. Many church leaders today are missing an opportunity to resist the cultural priority on individual leadership by embracing the biblical model of team leadership. It may be messier and less efficient, but the preference for efficiency may be more cultural than biblical. After all, collaboration exists even within the Trinity, as the Father, Son, and Spirit work together. Those of us in churches that focus on the Holy Spirit should and must find ways to live this biblical truth consistently, for the Spirit empowers not just a singular leader but all of God's people.

Paul describes his apostleship as coming about **by the will of God** (the same language appears in 2 Cor. 1:1). Some may understand this as highlighting Paul's superiority or authority, especially because Timothy is not described as an apostle. However, Paul's apostleship is an ongoing source of humble gratitude for him, an act of grace that is not deserved (1 Cor. 15:8–10). He is an apostle not by his own choice but by the gift of God's will; this shapes his life powerfully, including his many experiences of suffering because of it (for example, 2 Cor. 11:23–30). He likely adds the language of "God's will" here because he has not personally planted the church in Colossae, or even visited that community yet, though they likely would have heard of him because of his extended time in Ephesus, about 150 miles away. As he communicates with these brothers and sisters in Christ, he highlights the reality that God chooses apostles (beginning with the Twelve in the Gospels [see, for example, Mark 3:14]) and that the apostolic task is at least partly to communicate for and represent Christ, as Paul does in his many letters.

2. See, for example, Acts 14:23; 5:2, 4, 6, 22–23; 16:4; 20:17; 21:18; Phil. 1:1; 1 Thess. 5:12; 1 Tim. 4:14; 5:17; Titus 1:5–7; Heb. 13:7, 17; James 5:14; 1 Pet. 5:1, 5.

Those of us in churches that focus on the Holy Spirit often see the apostolic gift as continuing today, and there is solid biblical evidence to support this view. While some have attempted to limit the gift to the twelve apostles and Paul, the New Testament itself extends the boundaries for who can be and is an apostle. For example, Barnabas is called an apostle in Acts 14:4, 14; 1 Cor. 9:5–6. Andronicus and Junia (a woman!) are identified as apostles in Rom. 16:7. Apollos is included as an apostle in 1 Cor. 4:6–9; and many seem to be included as apostles in 1 Cor. 15:7, as "all the apostles" appears to be a different group from the Twelve mentioned in verse 5. James, Jesus's brother, is called an apostle in Gal. 1:19. Silas and Timothy are included as apostles in 1 Thess. 2:6 (see 1:1 for the identity of the "we").

The point here is that apostleship clearly extends beyond the Twelve and Paul. Some opponents of this view have argued that *the* criterion for apostleship is that one has to have seen the risen Lord, because of what Paul says in 1 Cor. 9:1: "Am I not free? Am I not an apostle? Have I not seen Jesus our Lord? Are you not the result of my work in the Lord?" It is more likely, however, that these are separate questions, not all qualifications of apostleship.

Also, in Acts 1:22 the qualification for the apostle to replace Judas is that he must have been with the disciples since Jesus was alive, "beginning from John's baptism to the time when Jesus was taken up from us. For one of these must become a witness with us of his resurrection." This was true for the Twelve, but if this were the key criterion for apostleship more generally, even Paul would not have qualified. In other words, various criteria are given, and it is unclear how and whether all of the people actually called apostles in the New Testament actually fit the criteria. Because of the way in which apostleship seems to open up, to include a group that is less and less exclusive, and because it is included as a gift in lists that contain other gifts still operating today (see 1 Cor. 12:27–31; Eph. 4:11), those of us who emphasize the Holy Spirit often see the trajectory itself as the point: there were twelve apostles at first, but after the gift of apostleship was established, it expands to include many, many others even today, including women. The work of apostles is never described comprehensively in the New Testament, though those who are called apostles after the resurrection and ascension of Jesus appear to travel often, with the goal of such itinerant ministry being to envision how the gospel can find rootedness in a new context and then implement that vision. They are, at the very least, those whose Spirit-inspired gifts include the creativity to see how the restorative work of the kingdom of God can shape a new city or province and then begin that important kingdom work. In other words, the apostolic gift is at its core a *gift* offered in service to God and God's kingdom and not primarily about power. This should caution us against abuses of power by those who claim to be apostles today.

In good form for ancient Mediterranean people, next Paul specifies the audience of the letter in Col. 1:2. He calls the Colossian Christians **holy** (*hagios*) and **faithful** (*pistos*). Both designations recall both God and the people of God in the Old Testament (for example, Exod. 22:31; Ps. 101:6), and both stress that such people *belong to* God and are dedicated to God's purposes. They thus should be faithful to God rather than to worldly leaders (such as the emperor Nero). What is most significant here is that Paul is using these descriptions for a church that appears to be largely non-Jewish rather than Jewish. Adopting Jewish language for the people of God formed in Christ, Jew and gentile, is a provocative and powerful statement regarding their identity, tying these new followers of Jesus into the larger story of the Bible and God's formation of a people to call his own. The divide between Jew and gentile is the primary ethnic and/or racial tension in the New Testament, appearing again and again across the books. The New Testament authors agree that gentiles are now included fully in the people of God *as gentiles* (without needing to convert to Judaism), and the ensuing tensions stem from the clash of various cultural and ethnic identity issues. But also, again and again, including in Colossians itself, the New Testament authors insist that these new churches must work through the tension rather than ignore it. They must learn to discern where to give space to those who are different from them racially while also resisting the easier and more efficient solution of separating into different groups on the basis of ethnic background and cultural practice.

Texts like this speak powerfully to our context(s) today. Christian unity must be maintained in local communities across differences of race and culture. Such

PENTECOSTAL INTEREST

The Multiethnic Reality of Holiness at Azusa Street

The modern pentecostal movement in the United States was birthed in the first decade of the twentieth century. Its gestation included various holiness groups and preachers coming together in revival meetings at Azusa Street in Los Angeles. William J. Seymour was a key Black leader, though the racial makeup was not just Black and white. The November 1906 edition of *The Apostolic Faith* writes, "Bro. and Sister Lopez, . . . who are filled with the Holy Ghost, are being used of God in street meetings and in helping Mexicans at the altar at Azusa street."[a]

a. *The Apostolic Faith* 1, no. 3 (November 1906): 4.

unity comes at a cost for everyone, as no ethnic group, even the most dominant, can then assert its cultural standards as primary. This may include the choices of music, of preaching style, of food and drink (including when to fast), of when and how to celebrate festivals (see, for example, Col. 2:16–23 and the comments there). Jesus unites us; that is the central point. We learn to sacrifice and compromise and respect racial difference even (or especially?) when it is hard to do so on points that are not central to the gospel.

Paul describes the Colossians as being **in Christ** (1:2; see also 1:27 and comments there). At the very least this describes a deep union between Christ and his followers. Paul also calls the Colossians **brothers and sisters** (1:2). The Greek word *adelphos* here can be used to describe both men specifically and mixed groups of women and men, as the evidence from this time period demonstrates. When Paul writes to churches, it is clear that he is using the language to refer to mixed groups, as he often addresses women generally in a passage and sometimes even names women specifically, like Nympha in Col. 4:15. Because of this, the sense is **brothers and sisters**; Jesus, as their older brother the Son, has made them into one family. Neither race nor gender separates them; Jesus unifies them. Many charismatic and pentecostal contexts attempt to take this point seriously when they refer to fellow Christians as brothers and sisters. My coeditor for this series, Craig Keener, routinely signs his emails to me with "your brother, Craig." Sometimes he even calls himself my big brother—a valid point, as he is older than I! I respond with the parallel "your sister, Holly." This understanding of family, as determined primarily by Jesus and not the typical markers, finds its basis in the Gospels, as Jesus redefines the notion of family (for example, Matt. 12:46–50). Early Christians like Paul adopted that framework and started to call all kinds of people brothers and sisters, including Jews and non-Jews, slaves and free people. The opportunity for us today is not simply to use the label but rather to live as if we are truly family. In healthy families members sacrifice for one another; they share resources; they respect and speak the truth; they forgive. My husband and I attempt to live this way in our primary Christian community, which is our church small group. We offer childcare, and my husband fixes toilets and sinks. We challenge, when appropriate, in the context of committed friendships. We forgive when hurt comes, as it always does in long-term relationships. May our churches today become known for the way that we engage in our Jesus-family. What a testimony that would be to a watching world!

In his greeting Paul also extends **grace** (*charis*) and **peace** (*eirēnē*).[3] A common Mediterranean greeting was simply "greetings," but in his letters Paul moves

---

3. Although the earliest and most reliable manuscripts of Colossians include only **from God our Father** here, the Textus Receptus (the basis of the KJV) and some others add "and the Lord

beyond the status quo to grace and peace, which for him are always tied to what God has done in and through Jesus. Grace is undeserved favor, and peace in this framework moves beyond just personal peace with God to include also the larger dimensions of interpersonal and even communal/corporate harmony in tune with the rest of the nonhuman creation, such as the fields and the rivers, as in the Hebrew understanding of *shalom* (see also 3:15; Num. 6:24–26).

Jesus's proclamation of the kingdom of God includes all of these aspects as well, from the individual to the entire created order. Those in Spirit-filled traditions have often emphasized the individual aspects of the Spirit's empowerment and indwelling to the neglect of the larger realities, but the time is ripe for a broader engagement with how wide and how far peace may in fact extend. Our world is desperate for a message of hope that includes not just a single person's experience of God but also the restoration of broken communities and even of creation itself.

Jesus Christ" (see the marginal reading in the NIV). This phrase probably was added to conform to Pauline usage elsewhere.

Thanksgiving to God and Praise for the Colossians

The next section is the thanksgiving, another typical feature of letters in this time. After the thanksgiving, an author often commented on a pressing issue, which means that Col. 1:3–14 is helpful in framing some important topics in Colossians. Whereas other ancient Mediterranean people might thank various gods, Paul and Timothy appropriately direct their thanks to **God** (v. 3). Their thanksgiving is also connected to the prayers that Paul and Timothy (**we**) pray for the Colossian followers of Jesus. Paul and Timothy **always thank God** *when* they **pray for** the Colossians.[1] The specific reason for this thankfulness is given in the next verse: the Colossians' **faith in Christ** and their **love** for **all** other Christians (v. 4). The NIV translates this last phrase as **all God's people**, though the Greek word is the same as that in verse 2: "holy ones" or "saints" (*hagios*) (compare NRSV; see comments on 1:2). In other words, there is a shared identity among Christians; all are "holy ones" and thus are deeply connected to one another.

The label "holy ones" does not mean that followers of Jesus are fine as they are; the intentional path of discipleship means that this identity needs to be embraced through lifestyle choices in an ongoing way, as Paul will describe later in the letter (for example, 3:1–4:6). Said differently, God's people are holy

---

1. It is also worth noting that prayer in the New Testament is typically directed to the Father through the Son. This means at the very minimum that followers of Jesus can approach the Father as Jesus did. At a very early stage, however, Christians began praying not just to the Father but to Jesus and the Holy Spirit, which makes sense if Jesus and the Spirit are also God alongside the Father. See, for example, Paschke, "Early Christian Documents."

because God sets us apart for himself, but we also must act in ways that demonstrate that we are set apart for God and God's purposes. Paul typically casts a vision (more of a "theoretical/theological" move) first in his letters before later giving details about how such a vision may be lived (more of a "practical/discipleship" move).

At least part of the function of the label "holy ones" is to guard against the Colossians developing a superiority complex; they are part of the group of "holy ones," but only part. Others legitimately belong as well, even across areas of difference that may be racial/ethnic, economic, cultural, or otherwise. The same is true today, and the challenge may be especially sharp for those in charismatic or pentecostal traditions because of the legacy of marginalization that many have experienced by other wings of the church.[2] In response to such slights many in Spirit-oriented contexts have reversed, or attempted to reverse, the marginalization by treating noncharismatic Christians as lesser. Perhaps the time has come when more and more in the global church will embrace other followers of Jesus well, creating a new and bigger center and reducing or eliminating the size of the margin. This does not mean that significant areas of disagreement are ignored; it does mean that forgiveness and respectful conversation oriented toward understanding are paramount. How we treat one another as Christians is a powerful witness to a watching world, and it is sad that we have often squandered our opportunities to demonstrate Christian love to other holy ones. Love in the New Testament typically is characterized not by emotions or feelings but by sacrifice and commitment, and its goal is redemptive, in moving us toward God's purposes. It is this to which the Colossian Christians and Christians today are called.

The combination of thanks (to God) while praying for others also gives much to ponder. First, prayer for other Christians, including those whom we may not know personally (as Paul does not know many of the Colossians personally), is important. And such prayer, for Paul and Timothy, includes thanks to God. These two other-centered aspects to prayer can and should challenge much self-centered prayer in our own contexts. The thanksgiving to God is stimulated by what Paul and Timothy have heard about the Colossians' **faith** (in Christ) and **love** (for others) (v. 4). The noun "faith" (*pistis*) can have the sense of belief, trust, or faithfulness. Here it extends beyond mere belief at least to trust,[3] for the Colossians have already been described with the related adjective "faithful" (*pistos*) in verse 2. Faithful people live what they believe; they respond to those they trust with appropriate behavior. In this way many Spirit-filled traditions

---

2. See, for example, Wacker, *Heaven Below*, chap. 12.
3. McKnight, *Colossians*, 92.

are correct in emphasizing holiness, or faithful living, as a marker of participation in God's people.

In verse 5 faith and love are said to be grounded in hope, the **hope** that is **stored up** in heaven.[4] In other words, this hope is the basis for the ways in which they trust Jesus (faith) and love all the holy ones. This hope is sturdy, not flimsy, at least partly because it is stored **in heaven**. The word "heaven" (*ouranos*) is used in the New Testament in two main ways: for what we today would call the sky and as a description of God's dwelling place, God's sphere. The latter is the point here, for God is safeguarding this hope, defined in the rest of verse 5 as what they have **already heard in the true message of the gospel**. The "gospel" (*euangelion*, the base of our word "evangelism"), or good news, is what God has accomplished through Jesus, which includes the grace and peace mentioned earlier but is not limited to them. More broadly, in Paul's time the language of "gospel" was used by heralds as they brought "good news," including when they announced that a new Roman emperor had taken the throne. Emperors such as Nero proclaimed that their gospel would unite the world under Roman culture and law.

This good news **is bearing fruit and growing throughout the whole world** (1:6; see also v. 10). Agricultural metaphors are common in ancient Mediterranean culture, including in the Old Testament, such as in God's instructions to Adam and Eve to "be fruitful and increase in number" (Gen. 1:28) and when Israel's fruitfulness was a sign of their obedience to God.[5] The culture of the Roman Empire used similar imagery as part of its claim that the fertility and the abundance that it provided were good news for the people under its rule. Here again emperors such as Nero claimed to be the ones who inaugurated a new age or kingdom. In line with what Paul and Timothy have already stated, the bearing of fruit is likely a reference not simply to belief but to a deeper trust that shapes behavior.

The **whole world** here is a common ancient reference to the broader Mediterranean and the Roman Empire, though obviously the good news is truly a global reality in the twenty-first century. This text offers an example of a figure of speech that must be properly understood. Taking the **whole world** language literally rather than from the perspective of an ancient Mediterranean person is to misunderstand Paul's reference point. At the same time, however, we can celebrate today the ever-growing global growth of the gospel.

The Colossians have **truly understood God's grace** (1:6). This true understanding is likely anticipating some of Paul's warnings about false teaching

---

4. For the connection of faith, hope, and love elsewhere, see 1 Cor. 13:13; 1 Thess. 1:3; 5:8.
5. See, for example, Isa. 5:1–7; 27:6; 37:31; Jer. 3:16; 23:3; Ezek. 36:11.

that occur later in the letter, and the notion of grace is what they now fully understand (also v. 2). Beyond the idea of undeserved favor, in ancient Mediterranean culture grace carried with it the connotation of a gift. In other words, God has graced/gifted Jesus (and what he offers through the

Defining the Gospel

In the Old Testament the verb *euangelizō* (compare the noun *euange-lion*, "gospel") is used in the Greek translation of Isaiah to indicate the proclamation of the good news that God was restoring his people and bringing the kingdom (see Isa. 40:9; 52:7; 61:1). The good news of the kingdom in the ministry of Jesus is the reality that, in and through Jesus, God is inaugurating a time of restoration. Many Jews expected that when God finally brought the kingdom, it would happen very quickly. Jesus's inauguration, a term that means that the kingdom has begun but is not yet finished, was demonstrated through the entire "Christ event": Jesus's life and ministry (including his healings, exorcisms, feedings, acts of jus-tice, teaching, etc.), death, resurrection, ascension, and pouring out of the Spirit. All of these are signs that God's final plan of restoration has begun. The challenge for followers of Jesus, from the first century to the twenty-first century, is to navigate the reality that the age of brokenness and sin is still present, but at the same time the kingdom of God has been inaugurated. Both brokenness and restoration are present, and we are called as God's people to participate in the restorative project of God's kingdom whenever possible until it is finished. The tension here leads many Christian traditions to overemphasize one aspect—brokenness or restoration—to the near exclusion of the other. In Spirit-filled con-texts there can be a tendency toward overrealized eschatology, or the notion that full restoration now is always God's will. This can be seen when Christians insist that everyone should be physically healed now, for example. The New Testament insists, however, that full restoration of everything broken will occur only at Jesus's second coming.

This gospel hope, embedded in what Jesus has done, is secure, and thus it stimulates the trust and sacrificial actions (as the "love") of the Colossians. The question must be asked: Is the security of our hope enabling us to trust in Jesus and our sacrifice for other holy ones today? Do we really value what Jesus has done and will do when the kingdom of God is completed and final reconciliation is accomplished?

inaugurated but not yet completed kingdom of God) to the Colossians. Gifts typically were thought to be deserved or owed to someone; what is compelling here is that the gift is undeserved. However, gifts were also reciprocal; if a gift was given and accepted, an appropriate response was expected, even necessary, for the continuation of the relationship. In other words, a gift given in Paul's day definitely had strings attached.[6] In Paul's letters the appropriate response—the strings attached—to God's gift in and through Jesus includes a lifestyle of following Jesus and becoming more like him (as disciples of teachers were expected to do), a topic that Paul will explore further in chapters 2 and 3.

The day the Colossians **heard** the good news is the day that **Epaphras** shared it with them (1:7). We hear of Epaphras only in Colossians and Philemon (Col. 1:7; 4:12; Philem. 23). He is the one who shared the gospel with the Colossians, which means that he helped to plant the church. Epaphras is clearly another coworker of Paul. He is compellingly described with "slave" language in a way that links him to Paul and Timothy. Though often translated as **fellow servant**, the Greek word *syndoulos* can be translated as "fellow slave," and in an ancient Mediterranean context, where slavery was a constant reality, the point would be powerful, as slaves were owned by others (for more discussion, see the comments on slavery in the introduction). Paul uses "slave" language elsewhere to describe his own labor for God,[7] and he argues that everyone is a slave to something or someone (for example, Rom. 6:16, 19; this is also relevant for understanding the "redemption" language in Col. 1:14).

It is popular to talk about "servant leadership" today, and many would use this term to describe their own leadership, or at least for a reality they hope to embody. Because many of us do not live in contexts where we witness the daily realities of slavery, the language is not as meaningful or challenging. How might ministry be shaped if we truly lived as if we were owned not by ourselves but by God? How would we treat those around us, including family, church, and broader community? How would we speak or teach? How would we spend our time? Our money? How might we share, rather than hoard, power if it is not really ours anyway? What impulses toward fame would be curbed if the charismatic leader truly was a slave to God?

---

6. See Barclay, "Gift Perspective." He explains, "Neither gifts nor the unexpected returns can be compelled (by law or force) without ceasing to be gifts, but they do carry expectations of reciprocity and usually are surrounded by moral sanctions (e.g., social disapproval of the ungrateful recipient)" (222). In other words, this critiques any view we might hold of "cheap grace" that allows us to live however we wish as Christians.

7. See Rom. 1:1; 2 Cor. 4:5; Gal. 1:10; Phil. 1:1; Titus 1:1. Tychicus is described as a fellow slave in Col. 4:7.

Epaphras is also a **faithful minister**, *diakonos* (v. 7). *Diakonos* is the basis of the modern word "deacon" and can also be translated as "minister, servant, assistant, intermediary." Epaphras told Paul and Timothy about what is happening in Colossae, including the dangers of the false teaching (which will be addressed later) and the **love** that the Colossians have **in the Spirit** (v. 8). The actual word "Spirit" (*pneuma*) appears only rarely in Colossians, though the Spirit's presence and empowerment are often implied, as it is the Spirit's work in us that enables us to live as God designed us to live.[8] While the focus is on Christ in Colossians, for Paul, the Son and the Spirit are closely related.[9] The love that the Colossians have **in the Spirit** is probably best understood as "love empowered by the Spirit," a common Pauline notion.[10] Even secular culture today encourages its citizens to love one another, but the New Testament argues that such sacrificial living is truly possible only when God's Spirit sustains it (for example, Gal. 5:16–26); no other power, meditative practice, or act of self-will is able to do so. In other words, humans, on our own power, cannot love the way that we are called to love. When we pray, could we ask the Spirit of God to empower us not only to love well but more generally to live well? In other words, could we ask the Spirit to help us see what we might otherwise miss if he does not prompt us to notice it, and then to help us participate in what God is doing in that space? Even if it costs us? And it usually will.

8. For example, Gordon Fee sees the Spirit as enabling the "power" language in 1:11, 29 (*God's Empowering Presence*, 637–38, 643–45).

9. Also helpful are the many references to the Spirit in Ephesians, which is the sister letter of Colossians and thus shares a great deal of structure and content.

10. See, for example, Wintle and Nicholls, *Colossians and Philemon*, 33; Fee, *God's Empowering Presence*, 638–39.

Casting the Vision (1)

Rescue and Inheritance through Christ

Paul and Timothy transition from the introduction to the body of the letter in Col. 1:9 (compare the overlapping content of Col. 1:9–14 and Eph. 1:8–14), and verses 9–14 stress key topics that will shape the rest of the letter. The past few verses have mentioned what God has already been doing among the Colossian Christians, and these next verses emphasize the hope of what God will keep doing among them.

Again the emphasis here is the way in which Paul and Timothy are consistently **praying for** the Colossian Christians. Consistent, urgent prayer is a theme in Paul's letters. I grew up in a house where my mom had a little plaque next to the kitchen sink that read, "Pray without ceasing" (1 Thess. 5:17). Her reminder impacted me, as I saw her actually pray regularly. She often talked about the content of her prayers, giving me a model for a prayerful woman.

The purpose for the prayer is that God would fill the Colossians **with the knowledge of his will through all the wisdom and understanding that the Spirit gives** (1:9; compare Eph. 1:17). Other Jewish texts connect the Spirit with wisdom and understanding (for example, Exod. 31:3; 35:31; Isa. 11:2; compare 1 Cor. 2:6–16; 12:8), including some that are not in the Bible but were widely used in Paul's day (Wisdom of Solomon 9:17–18; Sirach 39:6; 2 Esdras [4 Ezra] 14:22, 39–40). This is the second time that God's will has been mentioned in Colossians, as Paul is an apostle of Jesus because of God's will (1:1). Here in verse 9 God's will is able to be known through the Spirit; the Spirit gives the wisdom and understanding that God has and that we humans need. In other words, this wisdom and understanding are divinely sourced. It is possible that here Paul is again anticipating some of the false teaching that he will address more directly in the following chapter. In response to claims of secret knowledge, Paul here states that the Spirit is able to provide this knowledge, and not just to one of the Colossians but to all of them.[1]

Significantly, the purpose of the Spirit's work is that the Colossians' behavior may please the Lord (v. 10). In other words, this knowledge cannot affirm sinful or selfish choices but rather enables wise living and **every good work** (compare 1:6, 28). This is not a singular deposit of knowledge from the Spirit, for the end of the verse speaks of ongoing growth in knowledge. Thus, a clear focus on lifestyle is accompanied by a process of discernment whereby the Spirit shares more and more wisdom and knowledge. This is likely reciprocal: as the Christian proves faithful to respond to the knowledge they have received, the Spirit offers more knowledge, leading to more faithful living. This is true both

---

1. Bruce Wintle and Bruce Nicholls emphasize here the "personal and direct experience of God" (*Colossians and Philemon*, 35).

Black Woman Preacher and Prophet Zilpha Elaw

In the nineteenth century Zilpha Elaw (1790?–?) was an unlikely preacher in the United States. Scholar Lisa Bowens argues that Elaw saw herself not simply as a preacher but as a prophet because she depicted her ministry using language from 1 Corinthians where the effect of a true prophet is that "the secrets of . . . hearts are laid bare" (1 Cor. 14:25). Bowens writes of Elaw, "As a black woman in a slave state, divine operation of the Spirit in the form of prophecy validates that 'God is in [her] of a truth.'"[a] Elaw describes her ministry using Col. 1:13 as well: "The people became increasingly earnest in their inquiries after truth; and great was the number of those *who were translated out of the empire of darkness into the Kingdom of God's dear Son* [Col. 1:13]."[b] Elaw wrote her autobiography, titled *Memoirs of the Life, Religious Experience, Ministerial Travels and Labours of Mrs. Zilpha Elaw, an American Female of Colour: Together with Some Account of the Great Religious Revivals in America [Written by Herself]*, published in 1846.

a. Quoted in Bowens, *African American Readings*, 91.
b. Bowens, *African American Readings*, 91.

for individuals and for communities. Today we might call this sanctification, a topic that often receives a great deal of attention in Spirit-filled contexts.

In other words, this is a Spirit-enabled discipleship, and it was as needed for the Colossians as it is for us. On our own power we are unable to live as we are created to live; our selfishness will keep getting in the way. However, we can cultivate intentional dependency on the Spirit, and he will prompt and enable us to live in ways that are more aligned with God's purposes. We can cultivate this by asking the Spirit to help us on a regular basis (perhaps while we commute to work, while we exercise, while we cook) to direct and empower us.

At least two specific traits that the Spirit gives here are **endurance and patience** (1:11). The road ahead is long and hard, but the Spirit will provide strength. The realistic tone is followed by encouragement, as joy and thanks are stressed. These mainly non-Jewish followers of Jesus—as is true for most of us in the church today, who are not Jewish but follow Jesus—have been included **in the inheritance of his holy people** [*hagios* (see comments on 1:4)] **in the kingdom of light** by the Father (v. 12). Terms such as "inheritance" and "light"

PENTECOSTAL INTEREST

Understanding Atonement

Colossians 1:14 should caution modern readers of Paul's letters against adopting a singular model of the atonement. If atonement is what Jesus accomplishes to end human estrangement from the divine and reconcile humans to God (sometimes called "at-one-ment"), then here in 1:14 it includes the forgiveness of sins. Forgiveness of sins is often connected to what is called the "satisfaction" model of the atonement, where the central theme is the cross. Anselm of Canterbury (1033–1109) argued that humans are guilty of debt (sin) but cannot pay or satisfy it (as only God can), and justice demands that it be paid. Jesus can pay the debt (as God) and meet the demand for justice (as a human, for it is human debt, though not his). Some scholars, using this broader framework, specify that Jesus technically suffers *in our place*. This is known as the "penal substitution" model, but actually it is a subset of the satisfaction model.

But here in this text of Colossians the cross is not mentioned (though the parallel text in Eph. 1:7 adds language about Jesus's blood, a link to the cross). Paul uses a Greek word here for "redemption" (*apolytrōsis*) that is common in descriptions of buying back slaves. This is about God giving us freedom (properly defined as under God's rule). So, redemption is freedom *to* or *for* a new life in God's kingdom, but it is also freedom *from* the old life in the authority or dominion of darkness. The same is true for God's redemption of Israel in the exodus, which includes freedom from slavery but also for a new life (and also includes blood, though over the doorposts). This image is closer to what has been called the "Christus Victor" model of the atonement, which stresses that Christ is victorious. The central theme of this theory is divine conflict and cosmic victory over sin, death, and the devil. Evil powers keep humans in bondage and suffering, and Christ defeats them and thus reconciles the world to God. The theologian Gustaf Aulén (1879–1977) argued that this was the early church's main model, and it has been popular in many charismatic and pentecostal circles. The word in Col. 1:14 often translated as "forgiveness" (*aphesis*) can be used to communicate the idea of release; if release from sin is conceived of not only as a paying of debt but also as freedom, then the Christus Victor model fits well here.

Perhaps it is best to use both models, especially where one fits better contextually or pastorally. I have known many people who feel the weight of their sin; they carry it like a burdensome debt. The satisfaction theory could speak powerfully to them. However, others sense their sin and temptations to be a kind of bondage from which they need release. The freedom of the Christus Victor model could be deeply compelling for those in chains, as it was for the group Alcoholics Victorious, who were part of my hometown church. They insisted that the Spirit's power made it possible for them to live in victory over the temptations of alcohol, and they gathered regularly (as do those in Alcoholics Anonymous) to support one another as they attempted to follow the Spirit in this way.

recall Old Testament promises to God's people, as do "kingdom," "rescue," and "redemption" (vv. 12–14) (recall, for example, the exodus, where Israel is redeemed from the kingdom of Egypt and welcomed into an inheritance; see also Col. 3:24; Eph. 6:12).

The idea of being **brought . . . into the kingdom of the Son** is communicating the reality that the Colossians have been **rescued . . . from the dominion of darkness** and transplanted by God into **the kingdom of light** to be members and citizens (vv. 12–13). The dominion of darkness is the realm where the Colossians used to dwell when they worshiped other gods and powers. But this is no longer their reality; they are citizens of a new kingdom now. Ideal citizens embody the values of the kingdom to which they belong, so this stresses again the importance of living faithfully. On the other hand, they are not only citizens, for they have been redeemed from the authority or dominion of darkness. When slaves or captives were bought back for a price in the Roman Empire, they were redeemed. If God has redeemed us, this limits the authority of the darkness, of course, but the purchase does not mean that we are then free to do whatever we want. This is not freedom defined individually or selfishly; this is freedom to live as true citizens of the kingdom of the Son, in line with God's values.

Casting the Vision (2)

Christ as Creator and Redeemer of Creation

The first six verses of this new section in Colossians are often called the Christ hymn, and they contain some of the highest Christology in all of Paul's letters. The focus on the deity of Christ, rather than on his humanity as in a "low" Christology, recalls passages such as John 1:1–18. We do not know if Paul penned this or if he is simply using it; we also do not know if it would have been viewed as poetry by ancient Mediterranean people. Either way, the language is powerful in both style and content[1] and would be well suited for singing, as we know both Jews and Christians did when they gathered to worship.[2]

These verses demonstrate the ultimate reason why Christians should thank God. After just alluding to the exodus in verses 13–14, here Paul celebrates Christ's acts in creation (vv. 15–17) and the redemption of creation (vv. 18–20). The first line declares that **the Son is the image of the invisible God** (v. 15). In the Old Testament, God's invisibility is regularly affirmed but also linked to the language of "image." Israel is not allowed to make images of God (Exod. 20:4), but humanity itself, both male and female, is made in God's image (Gen. 1:26–27). Images were set up in the ancient world as reminders of who ruled an arca as well as to communicate characteristics of that ruler. Humans were created for this role (to be reminders that God is in charge), though Jesus is the

---

1. In ancient Mediterranean culture grand rhetoric was used in prose that exalted (various) gods or goddesses.

2. For example, the book of Psalms; in the New Testament, see 1 Cor. 14:26; Eph. 5:19–20; Col. 3:16; Rev. 4:11; 5:9–10; 15:3–4; compare Matt. 26:30 // Mark 14:26.

only one who can do it fully, at least prior to the completion of new creation. Jesus is the image and glory of God (2 Cor. 4:4–6; Heb. 1:3) and the one who allows people to see the unseen God (John 14:8–11), and being conformed to Christ's image is the destiny and goal for Christians (Rom. 8:29; 1 Cor. 15:49; 2 Cor. 3:18), a point that Paul makes later in Col. 3:10. Are we relishing the hope of being fully and finally conformed to Christ's image and considering even now whether we are bearing God's image well? Are we living in such a way that our lives are a reminder of the Creator's just rule in his kingdom? Are we witnessing to the reality of who God is and what God values?

The Son is also **the firstborn over all creation** (1:15). If we understand this as him being first chronologically, it can sound as if the Son was created first. The idea that Christ is part of creation rather than the Creator is the stuff of heresies, as in the view of Arius (ca. AD 250–ca. 336). It is better, then, to see Paul affirming that Christ is first in status and power; Christ has divine priority over creation. The following verse confirms this point, as it clearly states that **in him all things were created** (1:16). He is the Creator, not the creation. This is one of many texts where the simple act of reading two consecutive verses together, rather than one verse on its own, leads to a faithful understanding of a passage. It also coheres with Paul's teaching elsewhere (1 Cor. 8:6) as well as that of other New Testament authors (John 1:3; Heb. 1:2). The Old Testament mentions that wisdom is God's agent and partner in creation and instruction (Prov. 3:19; 8:22–9:1; compare Wisdom of Solomon 7:26), and the Christ hymn effectively places Christ in the role of wisdom, making Jesus the wisdom of God made visible to humans.

In Paul's day use of the language of "all things" was a common way to describe what we today would call the universe. This includes, of course, both earthly and heavenly realities. Though Paul does not define the **thrones or powers or rulers or authorities** here, the Colossians, because of their cultural context, would have known how powerful earthly powers (including the Roman Empire) are, and they would also have assumed that there are real spiritual powers that can both help and harm humans. Paul also uses some of the same language in Ephesians when he says, "Our struggle is not against flesh and blood, but against the rulers, against the authorities, against the powers of this dark world and against the spiritual forces of evil in the heavenly realms" (Eph. 6:12). In Ephesians the language focuses on what is clearly spiritual and heavenly, though of course heavenly realities often work through and influence earthly structures and kingdoms. Both are capable of rebelling against their Creator, even though they are created **for him** (Col. 1:16) and for his glory (and no one else's). Those in Spirit-filled traditions have tended to take texts such as this quite seriously, stressing that Jesus is stronger than all spiritual powers that oppose God and attempt to cause destruction in and around us. Interestingly, while many in Western contexts such as the United States and Europe have for years denied the reality of spiritual powers, the tide is now changing. At least part of the reason is a growing global awareness, as the majority of the world's population still understands demons and other spiritual powers to be real.

More broadly, this is a powerful reminder for all God's people in all times and places: even though the powers resist God's purposes, that is not their creational intent, and Christ has not lost control of them. For the Colossians this is likely connected to their fear and worry over astrology, as many ancient people connected the stars to gods and goddesses because they moved across the sky. A recent earthquake in Colossae would also have been seen by locals as not simply "natural" but involving spiritual powers. Whatever the source of our anxiety, Colossians resounds with the truth that Christ wins and other powers do not. Why fear the stars if you trust the one who created the stars? Why fear worldly powers of government or politics when you trust the one who created the powers? As my mom would say when faced with challenges of any kind, "Just say the name of Jesus. It reminds Satan that he loses."

After all, **He is before all things, and in him all things hold together** (1:17). We all need people we can trust, people who are reliable because we know they "got this," whatever it is. Christ has "got this" in a way that will be consistent to the end. The idea of "holding together" is communicating that he sustains and enables the permanence of creation. In my imagination I picture Christ standing and holding the universe. He kicks one leg out to the side, helping to balance the massive load he carries in his arms. Even though he stands on one leg, he does not topple or even waver. Instead, he smiles joyfully at me. He's got this.

Next Paul moves from Christ's role in creation to Christ's role in new creation. He returns to a familiar metaphor: Christ **is the head of the body, the church** (1:18; compare Rom. 12:4–5; 1 Cor. 12:12–27; Eph. 5:23). It was common in ancient Mediterranean culture to use the metaphor of a body when discussing the interdependence of a group, though typically it was used to encourage those who were culturally less important (as "body parts") to serve those who were socially more important (as "body parts") and thus further the communal body. In 1 Cor. 12 Paul subverts this usage when he argues against this hierarchical view by diminishing any sense of self-importance that some people might have because of their supposedly superior spiritual gifts. Paul argues for the necessity of all the gifts, including the "less presentable" ones, and in this way equalizes the gifts.[3] Here in Colossians, even though at least part of

---

3. For more extended discussion and references to academic sources, see Witherington, *Conflict and Community*, 253–59.

the point is that Christ **might have the supremacy** (NIV) or **might be in first place** (AT), our understanding of Christ's "first place" or supremacy is shaped by his sustaining presence. In other words, when we recognize that he is the one who holds everything together (1:17) and see him as our head (v. 18), we see the connection to our own heads. We simply cannot live without our literal heads (along with some key organs). Similarly, we as the church today cannot live without the sustaining presence of Christ. He holds us together. That is at least part of what it means for him to be in first place.

Christ is also **the beginning** (1:18). This language recalls Gen. 1 and John 1, emphasizing Christ's preexistence (and perhaps links with the preceding comment on the church; he is also the beginning of the church). He is not created

APPLICATION

What Does It Mean to Be the Head?

In Col. 1:18 Paul describes Jesus as the head of the body, the church. The idea of "headship" traditionally has been understood in terms of authority, which means that Paul is stressing Jesus's authority here over the church. I have often wondered about this notion of authority, especially what it means in practice. Does it mean that Jesus is in charge? That he is dominant? That he makes decisions? I know something about that; I call it "mom authority."

In every family I know, moms run the family calendar. (I am sure that there are families where dads run the family calendar, though I do not know any such families personally.) Moms schedule, plan, coordinate, sacrifice, sustain. Moms make those decisions. But this kind of authority is better described in ways that are much broader than making decisions. By managing the family calendar, moms give the family *life*.[a] They hold the family together (who, in this metaphor, is the body). It's a different kind of authority. It's not about *dominance*, or at least not mainly about dominance, but rather about connection and life and sacrifice for the group. In that sense moms are in first place. I don't think that this has to be moms; dads can do it too. It's really about the authority of the parent, the ones who create the family. Creators sustain, which is a certain kind of dominance, but a surprising one. My mom authority mostly looks like a sacrificial sustaining connection that holds the family together.

a. Craig Keener notes that "ancient medical literature sometimes described the head as the source of life for the rest of the body" (*Bible Background Commentary*, 575).

but is the Creator of creation. But he is also **the firstborn from the dead ones** (v. 18 AT; recall the use of "firstborn" language in v. 15; see also Acts 26:23; Rev. 1:5). In other words, in his bodily resurrection he is the first to resurrect, but he is not the last. His followers will follow in their own bodily resurrections when Jesus appears at the second coming to finish the new-creation project, when resurrection life finally and completely conquers death (see also 1 Cor. 15). Christ is thus the creator and sustainer of both creation and new creation; he is in first place.

If Jesus did not conquer death, then death still wins. But if Jesus is still alive today in a renewed body, a resurrection body, this means that life really is conquering death, as Paul argues in 1 Cor. 15. That hope can ground even the smallest decisions we make in life: what we do with our bodies (because God made our bodies and is not finished with them), how we treat others (as possible spaces for God to bring life rather than death), and how we spend our time and money (contributing to life wherever possible). If God is a God of life, will we risk our temporary lives now for the hope of resurrection life in eternity?

All of God's **fullness** dwells in the Son (Col. 1:19). Beyond expressing again the clear point of the deity of the Son (with a probable allusion to the temple as God's dwelling place), the language of "fullness" (*plērōma*) was likely used by the false teachers in Colossae as a way to stress that their special knowledge and experiences gave them fullness. Paul's point, in contrast, is that God's true fullness is accessed only through the Son.

The final point of the Christ hymn is about the reconciliation that is possible through Christ, and that includes **all things, things on earth or things in heaven** (1:20). Forms of the word "reconcile" (*apokatallassō* and *katallassō*) appear in several other texts in Paul (Rom. 5:10; 1 Cor. 7:11; 2 Cor. 5:18–20; Eph. 2:16), and they communicate at least the *initial possibility* of restoration of broken or even hostile relationships. Here in Colossians, reconciliation—also called "peace"—is tied directly to Jesus's blood and the cross,[4] a common feature (as I already stated) of a satisfaction model of the atonement (see the sidebar "Understanding Atonement" at Col. 1:13–14). This point also makes clear that such reconciliation is accomplished not by coercive forms of power but by the vulnerability and self-giving love of Jesus on the cross.

In other texts in Paul's letters the cross and reconciliation are linked, though in Rom. 5:10 Paul adds, "For if, while we were God's enemies, we were reconciled to him through the death of his Son, how much more, having been reconciled, shall we be saved through his life!" In other words, reconciliation is initial in

---

4. In ancient Mediterranean culture, blood was understood as the life force. This is of course important in many Old Testament rituals and sacrifices.

that it is accomplished by Jesus's death, but it is not final in that it has not yet been embraced fully by all who are "saved through his life," not just his death. Paul specifies at least partly what this means in Rom. 5:19: Jesus's *life* is one of obedience; being saved through his life links his obedience in righteousness to ours. In 2 Cor. 5:18–20 the point is similar, that reconciliation is available and thus true, yet these verses end with an urgent plea: "Be reconciled to God." In other words, reconciliation is not yet completed. It is "eschatological," a word that comes from the Greek word *eschatos*, "final." It has begun because of what Jesus has accomplished, but it has not been completed.

This makes sense when we think about the way that reconciliation works in human relationships. Even if a friend, spouse, or group (whether political, religious, ethnic, national, etc.) agrees to reconcile, a move that makes reconciliation possible, that is only the beginning. The process will continue as both parties build trust and communicate and invest in their relationship, making change together. The tension of this process also offers important context to the language of Jesus reconciling "all things." It is not evidence for universalism, where everyone (humans as well as spiritual beings, such as fallen angels) and everything (including the nonhuman creation) are fully reconciled and restored now. Rather, all things may be subdued, but they are not fully restored to their pre-rebellion state. The opportunity is available now, and has begun for many, but it is not finished yet (compare 2:15, which describes Christ's victory over the powers on the cross). Pentecostals and charismatics live in this tension, as we call on the power of the name of Jesus to protect and heal now while also living in the reality that demonic powers still do have real power to harm and that they can and do work sometimes through earthly powers like institutions, governments, and ideologies. Not all of us are protected, at least not fully. Not all are healed. Not all find justice. Not all are reconciled. Not yet. Someday we will see the fuller reality, and waiting in that space of tension is the challenge. How do we hold to the truth of what Jesus has accomplished while we await and pray for the fuller realization of it? Come, Lord Jesus.

The tension between what Christ has done and what still needs to be embraced/fulfilled in God's people continues in the next few verses, though here the shift is from the cosmic vision of the Christ hymn to the practical level of everyday life. The Colossians used to be **alienated from God and . . . enemies in** [their] **minds** (1:21; contrast the prayer for wisdom, knowledge, and understanding in 1:9–10; see also Eph. 4:18). This is connected to their evil deeds and can be understood in two ways. One option is that their evil deeds may have come first and caused them to be enemies in their minds, as in when people even today participate in sinful behavior without contemplating the long-term effects on their minds and hearts. The result is that their behavior ends up diverting their attention from God and creating enemy minds. A second option is that their evil deeds may be evidence for the fact that they are enemies of God in their minds, as when someone who appears to be a "good person" is shown to be false when their lifestyle choices are revealed. Perhaps both are true, and the reality varies by person or community. Perhaps only God knows which is the case in each instance.

Either way, the alienation is total rather than partial; minds and deeds are connected (as Paul also argues in Rom. 1:21–32), including in what we do with our appetites for entertainment, for power, for money, for sex, and so on. In Paul's day some philosophers imagined that people could be alienated in one part of their being without it affecting the other parts, but Paul is refuting that notion here. This is even more powerful when we remember that Paul and Timothy have already stated, "We continually ask God to fill you with the knowledge of his will through all the wisdom and understanding that the Spirit gives" (Col. 1:9). Such knowledge, wisdom, and understanding are the opposite of being alienated and enemies in our minds. Paul may be speaking about the false teaching in the church at Colossae, which could alienate more people from God, making them enemies.

Now, however, the Colossians are **reconciled** (again *apokatallassō*, as in v. 20) to God through **Christ's physical body through death** (v. 22). The emphasis on the humanity of Jesus strikes a chord in a letter so interested in his divinity. His physicality cannot be fleshly in a negative sense, because it is Jesus's body, and so at least part of the point here seems to be a correction, a warning against false teachers who would sideline or deny the humanity of Jesus in favor of a nonphysical preference, perhaps where Christ only appears to be human but is in fact not (a heresy known as docetism), or where Christ's divinity is elevated high above his humanity (part of Gnostic teaching, another heresy). Somewhat surprisingly, large swaths of the church today fall prey to these heresies, affirming a divine Christ but ignoring or downplaying his humanity. Such a low view of Christ's physical body often leads to Christians having a low view of their own physical bodies, which can manifest in unhealthy versions of self-denial. Unsurprisingly, this is exactly the problem that we see later in the letter (for example, 2:18–23), as well as in some Spirit-filled contexts today where Christians are encouraged to be "spiritual" rather than "physical." This can lead to sins in the area of food, such as gluttony, excessive fasting, and lack of concern for those without enough to eat. Priority on the "spiritual" rather than the "physical" can also lead to license to sin in other bodily areas, such as sex, as those may be seen as "merely physical" and less important. However, the New Testament and the broader Christian tradition both affirm the body as God's creational design and resist practices that denigrate the body.

A fully human and bodily Christ reconciled the Colossians, and us today, through his death for the larger purpose of presenting us all **holy in his sight, without blemish and free from accusation** (v. 22; see also 1 Cor. 1:8). Here the word "holy" (again, *hagios*) is used not simply as a synonym for God's people but as a reality that is true for those reconciled in Christ. Those who are holy, because they belong to God, are different or set apart from others in a way that is positive (rather than neutral or negative). This fits with the language of being **without blemish**, because in the Old Testament sacrificial animals were to be without blemish (for example, Exod. 12:5; Lev. 1:3); they were holy, or set apart, from other lambs and thus appropriate for sacrificial offerings.

Once again, the reality of reconciliation must be taken into the everyday lives of Jesus's followers, for this occurs only if we maintain **faith**/trust, are **established and firm, and do not move from the hope** of the good news that we hear and obey (v. 23). The good news or **gospel** is **proclaimed** everywhere, **to every creature under heaven** (v. 23). When we connect the "creation" language here to that elsewhere in chapter 1 (vv. 6, 15–20), we see Christ's commitment to both human and nonhuman creation. The question is whether we are proclaiming the gospel as good news for every living creature, not simply for humans. Paul is a servant or minister (again, *diakonos* [see v. 7]) of this gospel, and we should be as well.

Of course, the stress here is on *continuing*, which means that the Colossians are now maintaining that hope (even if Paul is warning them about the false teaching in their circles as well). Are we maintaining the hope? The word for "hear" (*akouō*) in verse 23 can also be translated as "obey," the result of true hearing. How faithful are we? And our leaders? It is the sad truth that many well-known leaders in charismatic settings have experienced very public moral failings (in the areas of sexual sin, greed, and abuse of power especially), where their sinful behavior illustrated their departure from the hope of the good news. Here again it is worth remembering Paul's commitment to team leadership and ministry as an accountable safeguard for all involved (see also comments on 1:1).

This text serves both as a comfort and as a warning to followers of Jesus today, and the warning may be especially sharp for those in circles that emphasize the Holy Spirit: an individual or community with "impressive" spiritual gifts, such as tongues and prophecy, may actually be an enemy of God in their mind(s) and be risking the loss of their reconciliation through Christ if their actions are evil rather than in alignment with God's purposes. Because many pentecostal and charismatic traditions believe that a person can lose their salvation (in some contexts the language of "backsliding" is common), passages such as this function as a clear warning to remain faithful so that salvation is maintained.

Casting the Vision (3)

The Mystery of Christ Revealed to Us

Colossians 1:24 has generated a great deal of discussion. Paul comments (speaking only about himself, not Timothy) that he rejoices in the suffering that he experiences on behalf of the Colossians, but he also says, **I fill up in my flesh what is still lacking in regard to Christ's afflictions, for the sake of his body, which is the church**. The idea of rejoicing in suffering, even on behalf of others, is familiar from other texts in Paul's letters,[1] but how could he state that he is filling up what is lacking in Jesus's afflictions? Is Christ's sacrifice not enough? If so, could we describe Paul's role as unique but also derivative of the role of Jesus? The problem here is that Paul elsewhere argues that Jesus's sacrifice is enough (for example, Rom. 6:10), including in Colossians itself (1:14), so how can we understand Col. 1:24 if we still view Paul (rather than someone else) as the author? (See the discussion of authorship in the introduction.)

The noun for "afflictions" (*thlipsis*) makes this even more complicated, as it is used elsewhere in the New Testament for the sufferings of Jesus's followers but not for Jesus himself.[2] Or perhaps the afflictions that are lacking are not Jesus's own but Paul's own. Perhaps Paul has not yet suffered enough of the "Christ-afflictions" connected to his calling and needs to suffer more, even to death, when they will be "filled up." But how would Paul's afflictions then benefit others, as he says in this verse? Could they be part of Paul's global mission, which

1. See, for example, Rom. 5:3; 1 Cor. 4:9–13; 2 Cor. 1:3–11; 11:23–33; 12:9–10; 13:4; Gal. 6:17.
2. See Acts 14:22; 20:23; Rom. 5:3; 8:35; 2 Cor. 1:4, 8; Phil. 1:17.

leads to salvation for many people, especially gentiles, whom he mentions three verses later (v. 27)?

Some argue here that Paul's suffering benefits others, including the Colossians, because he is taking on at least part of their share of suffering for Christ; he experiences more suffering than others do because he is so faithful as a follower of Jesus. Many Jews in the time of Jesus and Paul thought that severe afflictions would need to be experienced by God's faithful people as part of the ushering in of the kingdom of God, and Paul could have this in mind here in Colossians even if he does not mention it directly.[3] His suffering could then be seen as encouraging for others, even as it makes him more like Jesus. However, it can also be seen as slightly disrespectful. If other Christians—both in Paul's day and ours—are being sharply persecuted, is Paul minimizing their suffering by claiming to take some of theirs on his shoulders, as if theirs is not that bad or could be worse? Of course, Paul's own suffering was extensive (see, for example, 1 Cor. 4:9–13; 2 Cor. 11:23–33).

Perhaps the best option connects Paul's comments here in Col. 1:24 to an Old Testament framework, as Paul so often uses the Jewish Scriptures in his letters. In the book of Isaiah, God's "servant" (or "slave") takes center stage in chapters 40–53.[4] The servant is often labeled "Israel," which makes clear that God's people are supposed to embody this vocation. In some of the texts the servant appears to be either a smaller group within Israel or an individual who represents Israel and is thus faithful to God's call. Part of the servant's task at these points is to bring the larger community of Israel back to God, though there are other aspects as well, including being a light to the nations. This focus on the nations (gentiles) fits well with Paul's call as an apostle to the gentiles. The servant testifies but experiences suffering because of this testimony, though God vindicates the servant as well, proving the servant right. In Isa. 54–66 this figure develops into a group of servants who continue the task of the earlier servant, indicating that the number of people who participate in God's call is expanding.[5]

Paul in this way sees Jesus fulfilling the servant role *in an ultimate manner* (for example, Rom. 15:21 quotes Isa. 52:15), though Jesus's followers (including Paul) also carry out that vocation (see also Acts 13:47; 2 Cor. 5:17–6:2; Gal. 1:15; Phil. 2:16). Paul, in line with the book of Isaiah itself, sees the servant vocation as open rather than closed.[6] We might say that in both Paul's day and today it

---

3. These were sometimes called "woes" or "birth pangs." See, for example, Dan. 7:21–22, 25–27; 12:1–3; Zeph. 1:15; 2 Esdras (4 Ezra) 4:33–43; 1 Enoch 47:1–4; Matt. 24:1–31; Mark 13:1–27.

4. See especially Isa. 41:8; 42:1–7; 44:1–2, 21 [2x]; 45:4; 48:20; 49:1–7; 50:4–10; 52:13–53:12.

5. For more detail, see Seitz, "Book of Isaiah 40–66," 514.

6. This reading of Isaiah (along with its reception in the New Testament) has been argued by a small but growing group of scholars in recent scholarship. See Lyons and Stromberg, *Isaiah's Servants*.

awaits embodiment by the faithful. The question is, Who will take up the mantle and continue the servant's task?

If Paul is assuming the framework of the servant from Isaiah here in Col. 1:24, then one could see a "deficiency" or "lack" in Christ's sufferings in the sense that the servant vocation in Isaiah is open rather than closed. It was never intended to be embodied by just one person and must be continued. It is also possible that Paul sees a unique role for himself in this task, at least initially; his emphasis on his role as apostle to the gentiles may point toward this (Col. 1:27), especially because the gentile component is directly tied to the broader vision in Isaiah. In terms of suffering, Paul definitely sees himself taking on his share, and perhaps shouldering some of the shares of others. If the servant is in view, however, the reality that this was first Israel's calling strengthens the idea that this is not unique to Paul but rather is expected for all faithful followers of Jesus.

Many Christians today across the globe experience regular persecution. Their commitment to Jesus has a price. They lose reputation, money, family, safety. Could it be that such suffering contributes in meaningful ways to God's restorative plan? Could it be that such suffering actually marks those Christians and churches as true and faithful? To quote James Dunn, at the heart of Paul's suffering "is the double claim that the suffering and dying of Christ provides a key insight into the way that the cosmos is constituted and into its reclamation (1:15–20) and that it is only by identification with this Christ in the way of suffering that those who serve the church can help it truly to be his body, the body which mirrors the cosmos as it was intended to be."[7] In other words, we are deeply connected to Jesus in our suffering (perhaps we could even say that our suffering is the suffering of Christ) because of our commitment to God's purposes. Our suffering does not help us move beyond the physical creation to some kind of higher "spiritual" realm, as some Colossians may have believed, but rather is one of the ways that God works to restore the physical creation, including us.

If at least one of the ways that God restores is *through* suffering, rather than *around* it, this is a powerful critique to some pentecostals who insist that suffering is never God's will (see also the sidebar "Persecution Today" at Col. 4:3–4). It may not be God's end or ultimate will, but until the kingdom of God is fully here and global new creation is complete, suffering (because of commitment to Christ) is at least sometimes the path toward final restoration (which is when the servant's task is complete). And our suffering today can benefit others: while the servant suffers most famously "for" or "on behalf of" others in Isa. 53, other servant(s) texts also emphasize that suffering can benefit others in a variety of

7. Dunn, *Epistles*, 117.

ways (see, for example, Isa. 49:4; 50:6; 57:1),[8] including by protecting, encouraging, or providing for them. (I think here of limiting our use of resources so that others have enough and that nonhuman creation is not abused.) Paul, a servant (Col. 1:25),[9] proclaims this truth. He serves the church according to God's commission, with the purpose of being able **to present to** [them] **the word of God in its fullness** (v. 25, *plēroō* ["fill, fulfill"]; also in v. 9; see also Rom. 15:19; compare *plērophoreō* in 2 Tim. 4:17). This is all for the benefit of the Colossians ("for you" [1:25]), and for us, that we may know the truth. Following Jesus should, and will, cost us.

The full word of God includes the **mystery** (*mystērion*) that is now revealed to the "holy ones" (*hagios*) (v. 26 [see comments on *hagios* in vv. 2, 4, 12, 22]). When Paul uses the word *mystērion* (also in 2:2; 4:3) in his letters, it always refers to a reality that used to be secret (only God knew) but now has been revealed to humans in and through what Jesus has done. In other words, the mystery is no longer a mystery (see Rom. 16:25–27; 1 Cor. 2:6–16; 1 Tim. 3:16). It is also not the secret knowledge of a few elite people, which may have been what the false teachers in Colossae were claiming; possession of secret knowledge in these groups meant that some people were elevated above others. The mystery in Paul's letters is revealed to all God's people because it is now revealed publicly; all are equal because of it. The mystery is associated with God's inclusion of gentiles, not only Jews, in salvation (Col. 1:27).

The **glorious riches of this mystery** are called **the hope of glory** (v. 27). Paul has already discussed and defined hope. Earlier in this chapter he states that it is "stored up" in heaven (v. 5). This hope, defined as what the Colossians have "already heard in the true message of the gospel" (again, v. 5), is the basis for the trust and love that followers of Jesus exhibit. The gospel is defined by what Jesus has done, especially in his project of reconciliation that someday will be finished across the created order. He even now holds all things together (vv. 15–20).

---

8. Christopher Seitz stresses the vicariousness of the suffering of both Christ and Paul, and he sees as the Old Testament background figures including Moses, Elijah, Samuel, Jeremiah, Ezekiel, and especially the "Suffering Servant" in Isaiah (*Colossians*, 107–8).

9. Paul calls himself a *diakonos* ("servant" or "minister") in Col. 1:23 rather than a *doulos* or *pais*, the two words used most commonly in the Greek translation of Isaiah. However, in Col. 1:7 both *syndoulos* and *diakonos* are used of Epaphras, and in 4:7 both are used of Tychicus, making possible only fine distinctions at most between the two words (see McKnight, *Colossians*, 193). One might also rightly ask if Paul's Colossian audience would have known and understood this assumed Isaian servant(s) paradigm, especially because the letter does not contain a single Old Testament quotation. They may not have known Isaiah well enough, though my sense is that because so many traditions about Jesus were connected to Isaiah (evidenced by Matthew, Mark, Luke, and John), to understand more than the basics about Jesus required at least a minimal understanding of key texts such as Isaiah.

The **hope of glory** is connected to Christ being **in you** (v. 27; see also v. 2), similar to how glory in the Old Testament is associated with God's magnificent and often overwhelming presence. The key here is that the "you" is a gentile audience, not Jewish. The same is true for many followers of Jesus today, who understand the weightiness of glory in our own experiences of God that challenge and transform us. Such close proximity to glory—a kind of shared glory—is the future of humans who are in Christ, as Paul says later in the letter (3:4; see also Rom. 8:17). Said differently, the creational glory lost at the fall in Gen. 3 is being renewed in the participants of the new creation. This is made possible by Christ, not by the false teaching present in the church at Colossae (for example, Col. 2:18).

As Paul has already taught in Colossians, hearing or even knowing the word of God is not enough; the bigger goal is for people to be formed as mature disciples because of the wisdom they have been given (1:9–10). Colossians 1 concludes with Paul and Timothy reaffirming that basic point: **He is the one we proclaim, admonishing** [*noutheteō*] **and teaching everyone with all wisdom, so that we may present everyone fully mature in Christ** (v. 28). This verse critiques Christian proclamation that is unbalanced, that encourages or stresses only positive aspects. Admonishment, after all, is warning. Paul and Timothy use this same verb, *noutheteō*, later in 3:16 to describe how Christians should interact with one another, thus showing us that it is not only leadership who can and should give warnings in our churches today. Paul and Timothy also teach with wisdom (see also 1 Cor. 2:6–7); the Spirit provides wisdom (Col. 1:9), and this also depicts appropriate Christian teaching as being Spirit-infused.

They teach all people, not just some, with the purpose that all may be **fully mature in Christ** (1:28; see also Jesus's command to his followers in Matt. 5:48 and Paul's observation about the church in Eph. 5:27). Because all are not fully mature or whole now, as is obvious, the goal here is an ongoing process of discipleship. Again, simply hearing or thinking is not enough; mature disciples live as Jesus lived as they walk in his footsteps.

The language alternates in this section between "we" and "I." In the final verse of the chapter, Paul stresses, **I strenuously contend**; but it is not his hard work or his toil alone, as he emphasizes how he does so with **all the energy Christ so powerfully works in** him (v. 29). Could this passage be a new personal favorite of yours, not because you find it encouraging but because you find it realistic? The Christian life requires a great deal of our own energy, though we can pray daily that the Spirit would empower our feeble efforts. When we feel that we are in a battle or athletic competition for which we feel deeply unprepared, we must indeed strenuously contend. Can we remind ourselves that it is not simply our power that is at work in living faithful Christian lives, and that attempting to do it on our own power never works, because we are created to be in relationship and connection with God and God's power? May we be able to say, using Paul's own language, **Christ so powerfully works in me** (v. 29).

Paul builds on the theme of **contending** or struggling in 2:1 (see 1:28–29; related language is used of Epaphras in 4:12). He does so for the Colossians, those in Laodicea, and all who (like the Colossians) have not actually met him in person. He wants them to know about his struggle, probably at least partly because he will soon warn them about false teaching and wants them to trust him and listen to him. His stated purpose in telling them about his struggling, however, is to encourage them at their core (*kardia*, **heart**) as they are **united in love** (2:2). This first purpose is at least partly experiential; being encouraged in my core often accompanies a demonstration of being united in love with other followers of Jesus, especially those who have struggled on my behalf. In the church where I was raised there was a woman who deeply impacted my own faith and experience of God. She was there the first time I spoke in tongues as a child. She had prayed for me moments before. When I was in college and would return home to visit, she often found me before or after the service to give me a hug and tell me that she had been praying for me. We may already have been united in love, but in those moments I felt that unification deeply and was so encouraged by it. Experience is important and powerful, as those in Spirit-filled traditions today insist.

However, experience is not enough. Knowledge brings its own encouragement and is needed as well. Paul continues by adding another purpose: **so that they may have the full riches of complete understanding, in order that they may know the mystery of God, namely, Christ** (v. 2; see similar language in 1:4, 9–10, 26–27; 4:3 and comments there). God's mystery is here again linked to Christ, which seems to include not just who Christ is but what he has accomplished and will accomplish (see also comments on mystery at 1:26). The language in verse 3 might appear unclear at first: How are **treasures of wisdom and knowledge** hidden in Christ? Here is one of many instances in the New Testament where a deeper knowledge of Old Testament texts brings clarity. In Isaiah, God says that he will give to Israel "hidden treasures, riches stored in secret places" (Isa. 45:3; see also 33:6; Prov. 2:1–8; 8:10–11; 20:15). The purpose of this gift is that God's people will know that God is the Lord.

The focus here in Colossians is how the treasures are found in Christ. Christ is the one who demonstrates who God is, and this mystery is no longer hidden. We must *know* it, and knowledge is its own kind of wealth, as it gives security and stability in a world that often is in upheaval. In Col. 1 Paul says that wisdom and knowledge are given by the Spirit (v. 9), so what we have here is a powerful testimony to the reality that the Father, Son, and Spirit work together to demonstrate who God is, both experientially and through Scripture, in ways that humans can access.

Such a foundation is especially helpful as protection against false teaching, as Paul argues in the next verse (2:4). False teaching is actually a spiritual attack. True understanding and wisdom are given through the Spirit, so false understanding and teaching come from another source (see also comments on 2:5). This kind of attack often follows powerful moments of grace and transformation in our lives. False teaching is often enticing. Today it often proclaims, as was the case in Colossians, that Christ alone is not enough. In other words, at least part of the reason why Paul insists that Christ is ultimate in Colossians is to counter claims or practices that indicate he is not (see 2:6–23 and comments there for details; the claims may be explicit or not). Christ's supremacy or being in "first place" includes a host of related ideas, such as his role as creator (see, again, 1:15–20), so Paul is not defending the idea that belief in Christ's basic existence is enough. Our understanding of Christ today must be shaped by all that the New Testament declares about him; we must know the Bible well to guard against deception.

Paul's warning is just that, a warning. He rejoices that the Colossians are **disciplined** and **firm** (2:5), two words also used of soldiers in the ancient Mediterranean world. The use of military language here indicates that they are in a spiritual battle and must continue to stand firm; giving in to false teaching is not an option (see also Eph. 6:10–17).

Though he is absent, Paul is able to **see** them. This could simply be a figure of speech, but Paul adds that he is with them somehow: **in spirit** or "through the Spirit" (see also 1 Cor. 5:3; Eph. 3:3–5; 1 Thess. 2:17). The Greek word *pneuma* can be used of both the human spirit and the Holy Spirit, but it is helpful to remember that Paul insists that followers of Jesus share and are united by the Spirit (for example, 1 Cor. 12; Eph. 4:3–4).[10] Also, in some early copies of the book of Colossians, the word *pneuma* is written as a sacred name,[11] indicating that those who made the copy viewed the *pneuma* as the Holy Spirit rather than a human spirit. Paul seems to be indicating that even though he is physically absent, he is not completely absent; he is with them through the Spirit.[12] The truth of this is stunning. The same Spirit deeply connects followers of Jesus today.

I often ponder the implications of this connection, both positively and negatively. Positively, I wonder about the ways that the Holy Spirit unifies us. If we share the Spirit of God, we are linked in a more profound way than human

10. See Fee, *God's Empowering Presence*, 646.
11. Scholars designate these texts as 𝔓⁴⁶ (Papyrus 46) and ℵ (Codex Sinaiticus).
12. It is also possible that Paul is with them through the letter rather than through the Spirit. This would be a kind of "epistolary presence."

ties or decisions could make possible. We truly are one because we share the Spirit. However, our lives and Christian communities often do not exhibit this unity well. We are divided, and we act in ways that increase division rather than oneness. Perhaps this is one of the reasons why Christian disunity is so deeply traumatic, both for Christians and for a watching world. We are literally straining against the deep truth of who we are in and through the Spirit. Living "toward" unity (through intentional order and discipline common in the military, as Paul's language in 2:5 implies) does not mean that we must ignore all areas of disagreement, of course; it does mean that we must set as our first priority what is true through the Spirit.

Such union also cautions us against other forms of sin. Contrary to a typically Western way of thinking, the Bible teaches that our lives are not autonomous and private, and so what we do affects other followers of Jesus because they share the Spirit. In other words, how might our gossip, our anxiety, our pride, or our sexual choices affect other Christians? These kinds of sins are often connected to false teaching and spread like a cancer or virus through a community, bringing destruction rather than life. Tolerance of such sin can encourage a false unity, one that disregards sin to maintain the perception of oneness. Here is where regular teaching and preaching on holiness is needed in our churches, as it is difficult to call out such sin without regular public reminders of who we are to be as God's people, both individually and communally. Paul and Timothy will do so in Col. 3. May we listen well.

In the next verse Paul stresses again the sturdy faithfulness of the Colossians up to this point and their need to continue in this manner (2:6; see also 1:10). The verb often translated as **live** or "walk" here is *peripateō*, a word Paul regularly uses to describe one's lifestyle.[13] Those who walk consistently on a path soon find themselves living a life that is either heading toward God's purposes or not. Each step contributes to that process and shapes its final destination, making even small decisions and actions count. To use Paul's imagery, even a plant that has been well rooted needs consistent tending for it to grow in an ongoing healthy way (2:7; compare Eph. 2:20, speaking of being "built" as Jews and gentiles together in community). Also important here is a good gardener or at least a supportive environment that encourages growth, as followers of Jesus are not meant to be autonomous and tend only themselves. God and healthy community empower true growth for me (and you!) as I live "in" Jesus, drawing life from him, and follow his example, being continually conformed to his image (see Col. 3:10).

13. See, for example, Rom. 6:4; 13:13; 2 Cor. 4:2; 5:7; 12:18; Gal. 5:16; Eph. 2:2, 10; 4:1, 17; 5:2, 8, 15; Phil. 3:17–18; Col. 1:10; 3:7; 4:5; 1 Thess. 2:12; 4:1, 12; 2 Thess. 3:6, 11.

But what exactly did the Colossians receive at the beginning (2:6)? What were they taught (2:7; see also Eph. 4:21)? Many Christians treat the Greek word *christos* as a last name for Jesus, though it has its origins in the Hebrew word "messiah." A messiah is a human who is anointed by God's Spirit to carry out a task (which could include leading or delivering God's people), and Paul uses it here alongside the name Jesus and his identity as **Lord** (*kyrios*). "Lord" in the ancient Mediterranean world could refer to a human (including a master of slaves, a social superior, or the emperor himself) or to a divine being (many gods and goddesses were described in this way, including the God of the Bible). Jesus as Lord is God (and not simply a human man) according to the New Testament.

The reference in verse 6 to what the Colossians **received** (*paralambanō*; also in 1 Cor. 11:23; 15:1) likely points toward many traditions and stories about Jesus as God's Spirit-anointed agent, similar to what we find in the four Gospels of Matthew, Mark, Luke, and John. The faith here is not determined by each individual person, contrary to many contexts today where people talk about what Jesus means to them. Jesus may indeed mean a lot of things to a lot of people, but those realities must always be grounded in the larger truth of who he is and what he has accomplished according to the New Testament. And for all this planting and growing, this teaching and discipleship, the Colossians are to abound in thankfulness (2:7; see also 1:3, 12).

Casting the Vision (4)

Fullness in Christ as a Challenge to Idolatry

Paul next returns to a warning (Col. 2:8), and this one is reminiscent of his caution four verses earlier. In this way Paul's argument is repetitive and cyclical: he encourages, then warns, then encourages, then warns. Perhaps some preachers and teachers today will find Paul's style here to be helpful. He does not avoid the hard truth but intertwines it with the positive.

Paul uses the language of "captive." The Colossians are at risk of being taken **captive through hollow and deceptive philosophy** (2:8). The ancient Mediterranean world was very familiar with the idea of being taken captive (by conquering armies, by pirates, by slavers [see the military imagery in 2:15 and comments there]). This image would strike a note of appropriate caution and care. The philosophy is not a general attack on education, as is clear from Paul's own use of philosophical style, language, and concepts throughout his letters. In other words, a blatant anti-intellectualism, which is common in some charismatic circles, cannot use this verse to support its view. Paul is an educated man, trained in the schools (both Jewish and non-Jewish) of his day. The philosophy here is that of the false teachers in Colossae and is specifically hollow or empty; it is deceitful. This is because its origin is not Christ but human tradition and the **elemental** spirits of the world (compare 2:18–20). In other words, its origin is not only human but also demonic.

Paul's next comment affirms the idea that the "philosophy" in 2:8 is connected to the false teachers and negative spiritual forces or beings, for he reminds his readers and hearers that **in Christ all the fullness of the Deity lives in bodily**

form (v. 9; compare 1:19 in the Christ hymn). Genuine, appropriate access to the full reality of the divine realm is not through the *stoicheia* but through the incarnate Christ, who is God in concrete, visible, human form. The stress on Christ's body reinforces the idea that bodies are good and should not be mistreated, which is one of the problems in Colossae connected to the false teaching (see 2:16–23). Baptism, which will be discussed below (v. 12), also supports the goodness of bodies, as we identify with Christ's death and life—and thus participate in his fullness—in baptism.

Christ is the **head** of any other **power and authority** (2:10; see also 1:16 on Christ as creator of powers and 2:15 on Christ as conqueror of powers).[1] In other words, he's got this. He will not, cannot, be threatened by other forces, including *stoicheia*, whose "philosophy" is "hollow" or empty (v. 8) rather than "full," like Christ (v. 9). And those who are in Christ **have been brought**

1. The language of "head" also appears in 1:18; 2:19. See comments there and the sidebar "What Does It Mean to Be the Head?" at 1:18.

BIBLICAL BACKGROUND

Elemental Spirits

The elemental spirits (*stoicheia* [v. 8; also v. 20]) are sometimes understood to be the fundamental elements of the world, such as air, earth, fire, and water. The Jewish writers Josephus and Philo, contemporaries of Paul, use the word in this way (see also 2 Pet. 3:10, 12). Others understand the *stoicheia* as fundamental principles in an area of study (see Heb. 5:12). However, the *stoicheia* can also be spiritual beings (see, as possible examples, Gal. 4:3, 9), and this understanding fits best with the larger message of Colossians (see, for example, 1:16). Also, spiritual beings can work through other realities, including elements of the world such as water, principles in an area of study, or even governments and ideologies.

Today's pentecostals and charismatics acknowledge that some spiritual beings are opposed to God's purposes, even if others doubt this because of influence from the Enlightenment and its refusal to believe in what cannot be proven scientifically. An insistence on the reality of spirits has sometimes been the reason why Spirit-filled groups have been marginalized by other Christian traditions, though greater global awareness has highlighted the fact that most of the world's population today acknowledges the reality of the unseen realm.

to fullness as well: fullness began when they accepted Christ, and fullness continues to be the reality. There is no need for other (false!) teaching, as the Colossians were tempted to accept, in order to bring fullness. The false teaching is taught through various regulations and is connected to practices that deny the body (including fasting), the celebration of holy days, and the pursuit of powerful spiritual experiences such as visions (2:16–23 [see comments there]). Some of these could have been connected to Jewish practices, and some, to other Greek and Roman religions and philosophies in their ancient Mediterranean context.

The security of the Colossians is clear, with nothing to fear, as they are clearly included in God's people. They are **circumcised**, but not in their bodies (Col. 2:11), as was performed on Jewish boys on the eighth day (including Jesus [see Luke 2:21]). No, the new mark of God's people does not require one to become Jewish, as a new kind of circumcision is available through baptism (compare

APPLICATION

Fullness beyond Christ?

Even today many Christians are searching for a fullness beyond Christ, and many of us need a reminder of Christ's sufficiency in light of what other powers have to offer. Why fear or submit to astrology when we have given our allegiance to the one who created the stars? Our zodiac sign surely cannot give us the purpose and self-understanding that Christ can give. Why fear the *stoicheia* when Christ has not lost control of the powers? Any other techniques or practices we use to protect ourselves cannot compare to Christ's power. Why accept the notion, common in individualized contexts, that we can and should "self-identify" in every single area of our lives when the Bible tells us that God defines us? This may include rigid and defeating notions of our "true selves" and personalities, our intellectual capabilities, and our political loyalties. Why pursue powerful spiritual experiences, including those with saints, martyrs, angels, or other "positive" spiritual beings, as ends in themselves or in ways that prioritize those beings as necessary mediators between us and God? This last point is especially relevant in charismatic contexts, as sometimes spiritual experiences (including visions, being slain in the Spirit, etc.) become the main goal, rather than becoming more like Christ in our discipleship. Surely Christ's power is bigger than such powers that attempt to take us captive (Col. 2:8) by our own attachment to them.

heart circumcision in Deut. 30:6).[2] It still requires a "putting off," but not of skin or of garments, which were removed during some gentile religious rites (in groups called "mystery cults"); it is instead a "putting off" of the **whole self ruled by the flesh** (Col. 2:11; similar imagery appears in 3:9–12; see also Rom. 2:29).

We are back again to the idea that everyone is ruled by something; everyone is a slave to something (for example, Rom. 6:16, 19; see comments at Col. 1:7). Sometimes Paul uses the word "flesh" (*sarx*) to describe a human body without negative connotations (for example, Rom. 2:28; 1 Cor. 6:16; Col. 1:22, 24), but it can also be used negatively, to describe the sinful cravings that rule over a person, a community, or the world (for example, 1 Cor. 5:5; Gal. 5:16–19). At this point in Colossians Paul is clearly using the word negatively to describe sinful desire and even bondage (2:11; compare Gal. 5:24). Christ has put this off for those who follow him, and this "circumcision" transpired during baptism, which is a different kind of death and burial: not of skin and bodies but of the rule of sin and its cravings. This is the truth of how we have **been buried with him in baptism, in which** [we] **were also raised with him** (2:12). This is good news because death does not win; it is not the ultimate end. Life wins, and followers of Jesus have been raised to new life with him, both individually and in community. Our trust in the power of God to raise Jesus leads us to join Jesus in new life, and this starts as we resist the rule of sin that is defeated by Jesus but not yet fully vanquished from our thoughts and actions (compare 3:1; see also Rom. 6:4; Eph. 2:5–6). New life is complete when we join Jesus in resurrected physical bodies (see especially 1 Cor. 15:20–24; Phil. 3:20–21), when God is "all in all" (1 Cor. 15:28).

Baptism, then, incorporates a person into God's people; it brings us from death to life, from the death of sin's rule to the life available only in Christ. Paul elsewhere talks about what is required to be incorporated into God's people, and sometimes those requirements appear to be verbal only (for example, Rom. 10:9–13). What many pentecostals and charismatics overlook, however, is that Paul does indeed discuss baptism (for example, Rom. 6:4; Eph. 4:5; compare 1 Pet. 3:21). For him it is more than an optional activity to engage whenever it is convenient; it is instead a key way in which God works transformation in us, connecting us to Christ and the new life he brings in the kingdom of God. Such life was not possible in the old order, where powers opposed to God had jurisdiction.

Paul continues the themes of death and life (Col. 2:13), connecting death to sin (and the Colossians' status *as gentiles* with uncircumcised physical bodies,

---

2. This comment also helpfully tells us that the church in Colossae was predominantly gentile/non-Jewish.

Baptismal Equality

Practically speaking, baptism also points to equality, as both men and women are equally invited and able to participate in it. Unlike circumcision, which was only for males and thus in some ways prioritized them, baptismal waters are deep and wide enough to include women side by side with men, offering Jesus-centered death *and* life to all. As a student of mine said after studying this text in a group Bible study, "I'm on a high! It feels like a camp high! I'm realizing for the first time how powerful baptism is for women. We are included in the same way as men. This Jesus thing is really for us." She repeated this sentiment the following week, noting that she had often reflected on the truth and beauty of baptism throughout her time in class, doing homework, and at her internship. I reminded her, and the rest of the students, that this aspect of baptism coheres well with the truth of Pentecost, where God's Spirit was poured out on both men and women. We might say that the power of Pentecost is affirmed in other ways in the New Testament, including through baptism.

using *sarx* [see discussion above]). He connects life to Christ. The contrast is temporal: they ***were*** **dead**, and now they ***are*** **alive with Christ** (emphasis added; see also Eph. 2:1, 5). Sin, which brings death, is now forgiven (Col. 2:13; see also Eph. 4:32). The image that Paul uses for sin here is that of legal debt. In legal settings there is an official certificate or record of debt, and such debt condemns people.[3] Paul's point here is that God has taken that record **away, nailing it to the cross** (Col. 2:14), which is where the crime of the crucified person was posted. Jesus thus accepts the crime of others, taking their debt (2:14; see also 1 Pet. 2:24). For us the debt is forgiven or, in legal terms, canceled.

Here again we see what many people have called the satisfaction model of the atonement (see the sidebar "Understanding Atonement" at Col. 1:13–14). There is also a substitutionary element, as Jesus pays our debt for us, in our place, making this a key verse for those who support the penal substitution model of the atonement. One strength of this model (and Paul's legal language generally) is that it reminds us of the seriousness of sin. In a culture where we are often

---

3. From a Jewish perspective, such a record of debt would be connected to the Jewish law in the Old Testament, including sin and its consequences. Isaiah 1 offers a "covenant lawsuit" where Israel's unfaithfulness to God and God's law is the focus.

told that people are basically good, this text reminds us that even though God created humans good (Gen. 1:31), we are also sinners. We are both good and fallen, good and bad. Some describe our sinful condition by highlighting the human aspect: we were created, as humans, to live according to God's purposes. God's purposes make us fully human. But we all, from Eve and Adam on, choose to live according to our own purposes. We are then living in ways that are less than fully human. What we need is a fully human one who can include us in his humanity: we need Jesus. We need to be "in Christ" (to use Paul's language).

We need our humanity to be renewed, to move from death to life, as Jesus did in his crucifixion and resurrection. Pentecostal contexts are often filled with testimonies from people who are appropriately experiencing newness in Christ. Their prior lives of addiction, abuse, greed, and hopelessness have been and are still being restored. Tears are a regular part of such testimony time, and God is glorified and the faith of others is built up. The seriousness of sin is admitted, but the beauty of a canceled debt is celebrated, as it should be.

Paul mixes his metaphor in Col. 2:15, moving from a legal picture to that of military victory (compare the imagery of being "captive" in v. 8). This second focus is typically a feature of what has been called the "Christus Victor" model of the atonement. The Christus Victor model, as described earlier, emphasizes that Jesus wins (see the sidebar "Understanding Atonement" at 1:13–14). He conquers all forces opposed to him, whether human or demonic.[4] Here they are probably both human and demonic, in that the powers and authorities include both the Jewish and the Roman leadership who were involved in Jesus's crucifixion, as well as Satan and his minions, who stand behind and support the human and governmental forces opposed to Jesus.[5] As the Gospels make clear, and as Paul is well aware, Satan is the ultimate enemy (see, for example, Luke 10:18; John 12:31; Eph. 6:12). But Jesus triumphs, and boldly. He disgraces the powers by publicly shaming them on **the cross**. The image here would be familiar to ancient Mediterranean people. After a ruler conquered his enemies, he paraded through the home city (Rome is a good example of this) with booty and captives on display behind him (see also 2 Cor. 2:14). In this way the hometown crowd could see the evidence of what their army accomplished while away. The shame and loss of the enemies were on full display. They lost, and lost big time.[6] As N. T. Wright has described so powerfully,

---

4. Technically, God the Father is the one who is conquering here through Jesus; Jesus is not conquering on his own.

5. An Old Testament example of a text that describes a spiritual power behind an earthly one is Dan. 10:20–21.

6. The military imagery of a battle may extend to the following verses, as Paul does "battle" with the false teaching.

The "rulers and authorities" . . . conspired to place Jesus on the cross. These powers, angry at his challenge to their sovereignty, stripped *him* naked, held *him* up to public contempt, and celebrated a triumph over *him*. In one of his most dramatic statements of the paradox of the cross, and one moreover which shows in what physical detail Paul could envisage the horrible death that Jesus had died, he declares that, on the contrary, on the cross God was stripping *them* naked, was holding *them* up to public contempt, and leading *them* in his own triumphal procession—in Christ, the crucified Messiah. When the "powers" had done their worst, crucifying the Lord of glory *incognito* on the charge of blasphemy and rebellion, they had overreached themselves. He, neither blasphemer nor rebel, was in fact their rightful sovereign. They thereby exposed themselves for what they were—usurpers of the authority which was properly his. The cross therefore becomes the source of hope for all who had been held captive under their rule, enslaved in fear and mutual suspicion. Christ breaks the last hold that the "powers" had over his people, by dying on their behalf. He now welcomes them into a new family in which the ways of the old world—its behaviour, its distinctions of race and class and sex, its blind obedience to the "forces" of politics, economics, prejudice and superstition—have become quite simply out of date, a ragged and defeated rabble.[7]

A strength of Spirit-filled traditions is the way in which they stress the victory of new life in Christ. There is real freedom available from old ways and habits and spiritual powers. Pentecostals also know the tension that Paul is describing in Colossians. Yes, the evil powers are defeated, but that defeat still needs to be *worked out and lived* in the life of every Christian, every church, every community. It is true, but it must be embodied. Jesus, help us. Remind us that the powers are defeated. Empower us through the Spirit to live lives of victory—as you define victory—rather than defeat. As Percy James Bady writes in the song "I'm Free,"

> Praise the Lord, I'm free
> No more chains holding me

Paul next discusses what it means to live in a Christ-centered victory, and here we get a better sense of some of the issues in the Colossian church, including what the false teachers believe. Paul instructs the church: **Therefore do not let anyone judge you by what you eat or drink, or with regard to a religious festival, a New Moon celebration or a Sabbath day** (2:16; see what appears to be a similar though probably not identical problem in Gal. 4:8–10). The Jewish law is at least part of the background for all these topics, as it discusses fasting and

7. Wright, *Colossians and Philemon*, 121.

has detailed instructions regarding what God's people can and cannot eat, how and when to celebrate festivals, and how to honor the Sabbath. However, some non-Jews likewise stressed fasting practices in various religious settings, so the problems here cannot be dismissed as "Jewish issues." As mentioned previously, the Colossian church as a whole appears to have been predominantly gentile.[8]

It is easier for us to see the Jewish background than the non-Jewish, however, because we have the Old Testament to use in comparison. The Old Testament mentions fasting (for example, Lev. 16:29, 31; Pss. 35:13; 69:10; Isa. 58:3, 5), but Jesus does not teach that fasting is always acceptable, especially if done in certain ways (for example, Matt. 6:16–18; 9:15). The Old Testament gives extensive food laws that restrict what God's people can eat (Lev. 11), but in Mark 7:19 Jesus declares all foods clean. In Colossians Paul agrees and insists that Christians should give one another grace regarding what they eat or do not eat. He makes a similar point in Romans (14:6, 17). Verses such as these do not give Christians today permission to undereat or overeat (as food addiction, eating disorders, and obesity are problems in North American contexts) or to eat or drink only unhealthy options. The issue at hand is whether Christians can require everyone to follow various fasting or eating practices, whether Jewish or non-Jewish. Paul answers this question with a strong no.

The same is true of religious festivals, including the Sabbath. In texts such as Lev. 23:1–44 God gives Moses instructions regarding Jewish festivals and how they are to be celebrated (for New Moon festivals specifically, see 1 Chron. 23:31; 2 Kings 4:23; for examples of wine in ritual or holy settings, see Lev. 10:9; Num. 6:1–4). The Sabbath especially takes center stage in the Old Testament, including among the Ten Commandments (Exod. 20:8). But Paul again follows Jesus's lead here, as in the Gospels Jesus redefines the significance of various Jewish festivals along with the Sabbath and what it means to honor them. The Gospel of John is prominent in its theme of Jesus fulfilling the Sabbath and various Jewish festivals in the first half of the book (see especially chap. 5 on Sabbath; chap. 6 on Passover; chaps. 7–8 on Tabernacles; chap. 10 on Dedication/Hanukkah; see also Mark 2:27–28). Fulfillment in the New Testament carries the idea of filling something up, of taking it to the place it was always meant to go. Claiming to take a festival to its intended destination does not mean that its earlier stages were bad; it simply means that where it is now (in and through Jesus) is better.[9]

---

8. This is why Paul stresses in 2:11 that the Colossians are not physically circumcised and in this way remain gentiles.

9. Jewish laws that separated Israel from its neighbors in daily life with food, drink, festivals, Sabbath, and so on had the purpose of helping them stay faithful to God and not sin. Notably, though the New Testament argues that Jesus fulfills these laws, it largely maintains the moral expectations of the Old Testament (for example, regarding sexual ethics).

Today there are Christians in charismatic circles who insist on celebrating all the Jewish festivals according to their Old Testament specifications. They often insist that all Christians should join them or risk unfaithfulness. What this demand overlooks is Jesus's own redefinition and fulfillment of such festivals, including how other New Testament writers like Paul make sense of this redefinition for Christians (see also Gal. 4:10). It is perfectly acceptable to celebrate the Jewish festivals, though for Christians the extension of Jesus's own fulfillment of them should be included. However, that fulfillment also means that the festivals, and the Sabbath, are not required to be practiced in the Old Testament manner. The early Christians took this seriously and started gathering as the church not on Saturday (the Sabbath) but on Sunday (the day of Jesus's resurrection and thus the beginning of new creation [see Acts 20:7; 1 Cor. 16:2, and the references to the first day of the week, Sunday]). Jesus himself honored the Sabbath by healing people (for example, John 5:9–10, 16–18), which is of course a form of "rest." Perhaps Jesus's followers should take this broader definition of rest seriously and participate in a variety of restorative and celebratory activities when practicing Sabbath.[10]

Paul's point is not that food practices (including fasting) or religious festivals are bad; they simply **are a shadow of the things that were to come; the reality, however, is found in Christ** (Col. 2:17). In other words, the body that casts the shadow is Christ's body;[11] he is the reality, the final stage, the fulfillment (see also Heb. 8:5; 10:1). Recognizing the stage that we are in means that we cannot and should not simply live in the past; Christ has come. *Allowing* such practices without *requiring* them is a middle space, and middle spaces are notoriously difficult to maintain. It is much easier to be extreme on either side, for everyone or no one to do it. Paul, following Jesus, takes the middle way.

In Col. 2:18 Paul tells the Colossians not to let anyone **disqualify** them. In other words, there are actually people who are attempting to disqualify the Colossians by requiring such practices. Once disqualified, athletes cannot finish the competition.[12] They are no longer eligible for the prize, which for Christians is final salvation and full participation in union with Christ and new creation. Paul, however, tells the Colossians to refuse to be disqualified. The people who want to disqualify them are pretending at humility because of the ways they

---

10. Wright, *Scripture*, chap. 9.

11. Some English translations use the word "body" here instead of "reality." The Greek word is *sōma*. The argument about the shadow and reality is a philosophical argument that stems from Plato (ca. 428–348 BC), which again shows that Paul is opposed not to all philosophy but only to false philosophy. Paul is rooting his philosophical argument here in the incarnation (the Son of God becoming human) and eschatology (Jesus's inauguration of the kingdom of God).

12. Paul is a fan of athletic metaphors. See 1 Cor. 9:24; Phil. 3:14.

practice their eating and drinking (including extreme fasting) and festivals (including Sabbath). These false teachers attempt to enforce these practices on others, but their false humility is actually poorly disguised pride.

The **worship of angels** can be understood in two main ways (2:18). First, it is possible that these false teachers are actually worshiping angels, perhaps because they rightly understand them to be part of the divine realm and recognize their role as intermediaries between heaven and earth. Both Jews and non-Jews believed in angels or other divine or semidivine beings like angels. If this is the case, they are taking it too far by worshiping them (compare Rev. 19:9–10; 22:8–9). This cautions us today as well not to overestimate the role of spiritual beings, even if they are on God's side. We have already encountered the *stoicheia* in Col. 2:8 as elemental spiritual forces or beings who are opposed to God (see comments there). Only the three persons of the Trinity—God the Father, Son, and Holy Spirit—deserve worship. Worshiping anything or anyone else is idolatrous.

The second option is that these false teachers are claiming to have seen angels worship God (as in, for example, Rev. 5:11–12). In other words, they have experienced powerful visions where they have stepped into the heavenly reality (and perhaps worshiped with angels as the angels worshiped God). This probably is connected to fasting, as fasting is a common practice for those who see visions (for example, Dan. 10:2–21). They are bragging about their spiritual experiences and, while claiming to be spiritual, are actually demonstrating how unspiritual they are. It is this second option that connects powerfully to many current charismatic contexts, for there are those in Spirit-filled circles who claim special revelations and visions. Just like in Colossae, these visions today may be real, but they become problematic when they foster pride and are used as boundary markers that then disqualify other people. What do we do when not all have the same spiritual experiences? Do we rank them according to worldly understandings of importance and disqualify those who do not make the cut? If we do that, we join the ranks of those who, according to Paul, **have lost connection with the head** (Col. 2:19), Christ. As head, Christ sustains and nourishes the body of Christ, helping it grow; the body literally needs him to survive (2:19; compare 1 Cor. 12:12–27; for "head" [*kephalē*] in Colossians, see 1:18; 2:10 and comments there).[13] When cut off from this unifying basis, the body dies. In other words, Paul indicates clearly that those who engage in false teaching can cut themselves off from Christ.

As a teacher myself, I often ponder texts like this when I prepare to be in the classroom, to teach in a church setting, or even to write. Clearly, teachers

---

13. Craig Keener comments, "Ancient medical literature sometimes described the head as the source of life for the rest of the body" (*Bible Background Commentary*, 575).

will be judged according to a high standard (see also James 3:1), at least partly because of the ways in which we influence and impact others. The teaching gift is clearly not for the fainthearted. It requires discernment, careful preparation, reliance on the Spirit's power, and a healthy community of people who provide accountability. Pentecostals have a reputation in some circles for poor teaching or extreme views that do not have clear foundations in Scripture. Sometimes this is unfair, of course, as many pentecostal teachers assume the broader context of Scripture or are comfortable extending a view as long as the trajectory itself begins in Scripture. But sometimes the charge of false teaching rings true, especially as it concerns what Paul says here in Colossians regarding food and drink, religious festivals (including Sabbath), and visionary experiences. How often have pentecostals stated or implied that to be truly spiritual and reach the highest heights such visions are required? That eating or fasting is necessary? That Sabbath must be practiced in a certain manner? The fact that such instruction is often framed as encouragement (for example, "I'm just trying to help") and given from a posture of feigned humility makes it even worse. Again, the middle path is best here. Paul, for example, had experienced many of his own visions (see, for example, Acts 9:1–6; 2 Cor. 12:1–10). They are valid, but they cannot be a requirement. To disqualify others on this basis is to disqualify oneself.

In the final verses of Col. 2 Paul returns again to his theme of death in and through Christ. Here death is to **the elemental spiritual forces of this world**, the *stoicheia* (v. 20; see comments on 2:8 and the sidebar "Elemental Spirits" there). Again, death with Christ ends with life (v. 12). Paul is puzzled here that some may have separated from the spiritual forces opposed to Christ but live as though they are still connected to those forces. In other words, why might a person still submit to the rules of the world that are backed by the *stoicheia* and participate in death rather than life?

Paul just mentioned how the false teachers experience visions and disqualify others if they do not have similar encounters. This community clearly prioritizes what we might call "mystical" or "ecstatic" or "Holy Spirit" experiences, experiences beyond rational explanation. When we read this whole section of Col. 2 together rather than in pieces, what we see is that these "regulations" or "rules" are spiritually supported and thus have spiritual consequences. Some of the regulations appear to be partly Jewish (see especially v. 16 with the reference to Sabbath), though other rules could be non-Jewish in origin (as non-Jews also practiced fasting). We see some slogans, or perhaps some caricatures of slogans, for these regulations in the following verse: **"Do not handle! Do not taste! Do not touch!"** (v. 21). In other words, if you would like to eat or drink that, don't even think about it. Fasting denies food and/or drink, of course, but in the Old

Testament even touching can bring impurity or uncleanness and appropriate judgment (for example, Lev. 5:3; 11:1–47; 13:45–52; Num. 19:11–22).

These rules all concern **things that are all destined to perish with use** (v. 22), which probably means that food and drink are, in a sense, destroyed after eating and drinking (compare Mark 7:18–19). They have served their purpose; they perish (see also 1 Cor. 6:13). The rules also **are based on merely human commands and teachings** (v. 22). Here Paul comes close to quoting the last phrase of Isa. 29:13, which Jesus also quotes in Matt. 15:9 (see also Titus 1:14). In Isaiah God is critiquing Israel:

> These people come near to me with their mouth
>   and honor me with their lips,
>   but their hearts are far from me.
> Their worship of me
>   is based on *merely human rules they have been taught*.[14]

The last line uses (in the Greek translation of the Hebrew text) some of the same vocabulary that Paul uses in Col. 2:22, but in a different order. In Isaiah the issue is the misuse of the Jewish law; they are missing the bigger point and heart of it.

We seem to have a similar situation in Colossians, as some people are following various "religious" regulations—whether Jewish or non-Jewish—but actually have hearts far from God. Their quest for spiritual superiority in *how they engage* food and drink, fasting, festivals, and visions is misguided in that it cuts them off from Jesus (2:19). It actually reverts them to their pre-Jesus life because it allows the *stoicheia*—spiritual forces who are opposed to God—to rule them.

These rules appear to be wise because they look religiously mature; those who follow the rules seem to be humble and demonstrate appropriate self-control (2:23). In fact, Paul says, the opposite is true! The rules point to spiritual immaturity, pride, and inappropriate treatment of the body. They actually lack the ability to truly disciple Christians in appropriate ways of living that resist sinful pleasures, or **sensual indulgence** ("indulgence of the *sarx*" [see comments at 2:11; compare with 3:1–17 for true restraint and growth in maturity]). These rules are unable to disciple people well because only immature people need rules that teach them *not* to do things. After all, this is how we teach young children: "Don't touch the stove"; "Don't hit your sister"; "Don't sit on the cat." As children grow and mature, we teach the positive side of rules, which includes learning to use the stove well and treating both humans and animals appropriately. There is a big difference between not hitting one's sister and actually treating her in

---

14. Italics here and elsewhere in Scripture quotations have been added for emphasis.

ideal ways, and that is the point. In other words, we can technically follow the rule by not hitting our sister but still treat her poorly in other ways and thus be living far from the ideal. A lifestyle of growing in maturity means that one moves closer and closer to the ideal, but it can take a long time.

In a similar way, we who are growing in maturity follow Jesus in a lifestyle empowered by the Spirit; we live *toward* God's goal for us, not only *against* what the world offers. Fasting is productive, then, only if a larger goal is being pursued. Simply not eating as a sign of holiness is not enough and can actually end up as an idol in our lives (as many seemingly good practices or liturgies can), especially if part of the point is that we want others to notice how holy we are. What are we training our bodies, and ourselves, to do, positively speaking? To be? And how do such practices point toward the goodness of the body (along with the rest of the created order) rather than treat it as something inherently sinful or bad, as in various heresies? In other words, what does it mean for us to live out our baptism well, in dying and rising with Christ (2:12)?

Paul begins chapter 3 with a reminder: the Colossians already **have been raised with Christ** (3:1; see also 2:12; Rom. 6:5).[15] Even if this statement is phrased as a possibility rather than a reality, as in some English translations (for example, "If you have been raised . . ."), the answer is assumed to be yes, and so the next phrase is important. It tells us what we should do because we have already been raised with Christ. In other words, we have been raised, so we must seek "above" realities. This is because Christ is there, seated at God's right hand, as Col. 3:1 and the entire New Testament make so clear.[16] Christ's throne also challenges, of course, any notions that a Roman emperor (like Nero) or an American president are truly in charge. We are to think about and focus on things connected to where Christ is, **not on earthly things** (v. 2). Thinking about the right things takes discipline and the empowerment of the Holy Spirit. Could we ask the Spirit to guard our minds and protect us from thoughts that will distract or harm us? If we need to "get out of our heads," could we talk with a friend or spouse, trusting that the Spirit can use their companionship to reorient our thoughts?

In the Bible "above" and "below," or "heavenly" and "earthly," are used similarly to the way that the word *sarx* is used (see comments at 2:11). In other words, in some texts what is above is above literally, as in a tall tree or

15. Paul often spends the first part of a letter casting a vision for what Jesus has accomplished and then in the second part shows how Christians live the truth of that accomplishment in the daily practicalities of real life.

16. See, for example, Acts 2:33–35 (quoting Ps. 110:1); Eph. 1:20; Heb. 1:3, 13; 10:12–13; 1 Pet. 3:22; Rev. 3:21. Craig Keener details how ancient Jewish mystics focused on God's heavenly throne and some Greco-Roman philosophers stressed a heavenly perspective (*Mind of the Spirit*, chap. 8). Paul is teaching a similar idea here, though he focuses on Christ.

building. What is below is simply lower, like the ground. This does not mean that the ground is worse or that creation itself is bad because it is material; it simply means that some things are lower than other things. In other texts the point of saying that something is above is to talk not simply about height but about what is better. Higher is better and lower is worse, as in the way many games keep score. Paul is using the language of "above" and "earthly" in this second way: "above" things are better, whereas "earthly" things are worse. He is not talking about the physical creation being bad, since he has already established the goodness of bodies (in Christ's role as creator [1:16–17] and in Christ's body [1:22; 2:9]). Even if we understand Christ as literally being "above" right now, it's important to remember that the New Testament teaches that heaven and earth will someday merge (Rev. 21–22), which means that heaven will not be "above" forever but rather "below" *with us* as we live in full and complete access and intimacy with all three persons of the Trinity and with one another.

The point is that we should not think about and seek things that the world values that are opposed to God's purposes. Paul will explain what is "above" a bit later in the chapter (3:12–17; compare Phil. 4:8–9); he will also confirm that "earthly" things are sinful impulses and cravings (starting at Col. 3:5). This is important, as the false teachers in Colossae seem to have had a lower view of the body, seeing it as lesser or even bad and evil in comparison to "spiritual" things. They promoted practices that deny the body and prioritize visions (see 2:16–23), as many charismatics do today. Again, practices such as fasting and experiences of visions can be appropriate, but they are also easily misused.

Paul responds to this with a reminder that our future lives are connected to a very grounded, physical hope in Christ. This is not an escapist mentality

PENTECOSTAL INTEREST

Battling Negative Thoughts

A host of pentecostal and charismatic voices today offer resources on how to wage war (and win!) over thoughts that do not honor Christ. A popular example is Joyce Meyer's *Battlefield of the Mind: Winning the Battle in Your Mind*. While not all agree with her broader views on Christian faith, the influence of the book is indisputable, as it has sold millions of copies. It also showcases the pragmatic discipleship that is common in circles that identify as Spirit-filled.

that hopes someday to leave God's good creation. We have died (compare 2:12; see also Rom. 6:2; 2 Cor. 5:14), but our lives are **hidden with Christ in God** (Col. 3:3; compare 1:26; 2:2–3); Christ is our very **life** (3:4; see also Gal. 2:20). In other words, our future is secure, hidden and protected from any powers that may try to undermine it (see Col. 2:8, 20), and connected deeply to Christ's own (present and) future. What is hidden is thus not some mystery that only special leaders know and understand, as some of the false teachers seem to be advocating (perhaps on the basis of Gnostic or "mystery cult" beliefs), but rather is a truth that is revealed and known to all followers of Jesus (though often confusing to non-Christians). Paul here picks up on a common New Testament theme that stresses what will happen when Jesus is revealed at the second coming. He says that when Christ appears, we **also will appear with him in glory** (v. 4). What is hidden now—our future life—will be revealed in its fullness, and that will occur when Christ himself is revealed at the second coming. Christ's appearance in bodily (resurrected) form will match our own bodily resurrected forms (see also 1 Cor. 15; Phil. 3:21; 1 John 3:2), and it will be glorious. It will be impressive. It will metaphorically knock us over with the sheer weight of it. It will affirm the goodness of Christ's own body and ours. It will fully demonstrate the goodness of physical creation (Gen. 1:31) as God redeems and restores it, ending suffering (including addiction, depression, sickness, and other weaknesses of current bodies) forever.

I often imagine this scene when I hear the lyrics of the Bethel Music song "You Came (Lazarus)."[17] The song is about Lazarus, whom Jesus raised from the dead (John 11). But of course Lazarus's resurrection is a preview of Jesus's own resurrection, as Jesus's resurrection is a preview of our own when Jesus appears. The lyrics include the following:

> I'm not afraid, I see Your face, I am alive
> You came, I knew that You would come

I often imagine what it was like to be Lazarus. What would it feel like to be called out of the grave by your close friend Jesus? When we see Jesus in his resurrected body someday—whenever that is—I believe that I will think, "I knew you'd come! I knew it! I trusted that you would, and you did. I literally bet my life on this hope, that someday I'd actually see you and be able to hug you. Jesus, it's so good to see you!" Seeing someone in person is obviously better than talking on the phone (or in prayer) to them. We all know that to be true.

17. Written by Melissa Helser, Jonathan David Helser, and Ed Cash.

We are created to be in that kind of physical proximity and relationship with others, and not just human others but God as well. This kind of physical, bodily hope is at the core of Christian faith, and I cannot wait to see Jesus. I apologize in advance if I accidentally push you while I run to Jesus for a great big hug. It will be the best day ever.

Embodying the Reality (1)

Resisting Vices and Embodying Virtues

With the hope of seeing the resurrected Christ (and visions of hugs!) fully in view, Paul now explains how we should live while we wait. Resurrection hope does not mean that we sit passively or, worse, that we do whatever we want; rather, it means that we live toward our future. We live in line with God's values, with how Christ lived and still lives. We have died with Christ, and we must **put to death** all actions and lifestyles that are connected to our sinful desires and thus are earthly rather than heavenly (3:5; see also Rom. 6:2; Eph. 4:22). This includes **sexual immorality**, which here translates the Greek word *porneia*. *Porneia* is the root of the English word "pornography," but in the New Testament it is used as a catchall term to describe all sex outside the context of marriage.[1] Along with sex outside of marriage, other types of **impurity** and **lust** are also inappropriate for God's people. Both of these probably are sexual in nature. Today we might think of things such as pornography, hook-up culture, sexual abuse, and sexual relationships with multiple partners. In some ways *porneia* is the umbrella term and covers everything (except sexual abuse within marriage, which is sinful because it is destructive and dehumanizing), so that here Paul's stacking of closely connected terms is meant to have a striking effect on us. The effect is like being hit again and again on the head. We notice. We react. Here we are supposed to think, "Wow! That's a lot of sexual sin. God clearly cares about that." And if we think carefully, we realize that even "individual"

---

1. See, for example, Matt. 5:32; 1 Cor. 5:1; 6:18; 2 Cor. 12:21; Gal. 5:19; 1 Thess. 4:3–4; compare the related noun *pornos* in Heb. 13:4.

sexual sin affects the larger community, as misdirected sexuality strains current relationships and prevents the building of new ones that align with God's intent for humans.

In Christian community we need to resist the extremes of an "anything goes" sexual mentality on the one side and a narrow purity culture on the other. The former is clearly out of line with God's good intentions for our human bodies, while the latter tends to absolutize the value of sexual purity. Our sexual choices do not forever "ruin" us; forgiveness and a fresh start in Jesus are always on the table. An argument can be made that certain aspects of modesty in dress are appropriate, but direction should be given to both women and men (not just women), as both are morally responsible and capable of discipleship. "Boys will be boys" is not helpful or biblical when discussing sexuality; we are all held to the same standard in Christ. In other words, sexuality, like everything else in our lives, is an ongoing part of our discipleship. This is true not only for single people but also for those who are married.

It is not just sex that is the focus here, as the next two items in the list indicate other realities that must be put to death: **evil desires and greed, which is idolatry** (3:5; see also Eph. 5:3, 5). These were often viewed by Jews as typical vices of non-Jews (as Jews were well known in the ancient Mediterranean world for their narrow sexual boundaries and condemnation of idolatry especially). **Evil desires** may be another umbrella term that covers everything we feel like doing that is opposed to what God wants us to do, or it could perhaps be connected to inappropriate sexual desire that is encouraged rather than put to death. **Greed** is a more specific instance of that desire: greedy people desire to have more. Always more, because enough is never enough. Some people think that this is a greed for sexual pleasure, though the word is often connected to money and what money buys. Paul then calls it what it truly is: **idolatry**. Idolatry, or the worship of idols, is humanity's primary sin in both the Old and New Testaments (for example, Exod. 20:3–4; Rom. 1:18–32; compare Matt. 6:24). It prioritizes and gives allegiance to something that is not God. Allegiance to sex, to money, to ourselves—to *more*—is idolatry. If we live in contexts that are wealthy by global standards, even if we do not personally feel very wealthy, do we feel the pinch of a text like this? Where is our true allegiance? Does our lifestyle prove that our allegiance is with God, or does it prove that it is somewhere else, like money? If our relationship with money is never neutral,[2] then the question we need to ask here is about the current slant of our relationship to money: Is it healthy or trending toward idolatry?

God judges idolatry. The Old Testament makes that clear again and again, and here in Colossians Paul reminds us one more time: **the wrath of God is coming**

2. Green, *Gospel of Luke*, 596.

(3:6; see also Rom. 1:18; Eph. 5:6).[3] Typically, pentecostals and charismatics are willing to talk about God's wrath, or God's judgment, even though some other Christians today avoid the topic. In contexts like the United States this avoidance is at least partly because of the societal value on inclusion. Inclusion is seen by many nonfaith people and even some Christians as of the highest value. Anyone or anything that excludes is then committing a terrible social "sin," as they are defying the social expectation. To avoid the topic of God's wrath and judgment in Scripture, however, is problematic for a number of reasons: it misuses Scripture, defers to cultural norms rather than biblical norms, and misshapes discipleship in its refusal to warn us appropriately. The idea of a God who never judges is a scary thought, for if God does not judge, this means that all the evil in the world, from the evil in our own hearts and actions to that of communities, societies, and governments, will never be addressed. We all want evil to be answered in some way, and for those who consistently resist God's purposes, the answer will be judgment.

Christians are different, however, as Paul says that Christians are no longer that kind of people. We are called to continue our growth in holiness, to walk behind Jesus and become more and more like him. Paul makes this distinction when he says to the Colossians, **You used to walk in these ways, in the life you once lived** (3:7).[4] The ongoing nature of sinful lifestyles is the focus here. As above (2:6), "walking" language is used for how people *are living* in an ongoing sense. Recognizing this is helpful for understanding how lists like this function in Paul's argument.

Here in Col. 3 Paul commands the Colossians, **Now you must also rid yourselves of all such things as these: anger, rage, malice, slander, and filthy language from your lips. Do not lie to each other** (vv. 8–9; see also Eph. 4:22–32). Paul is acknowledging the tension here, once again, between what Christ has already accomplished (death to sin!) and how that accomplishment is formed in the lives of Christians. It requires that Christians continually set these sins down so that they live in more and more freedom; discipleship means that the desire to sin must not be embraced but instead be resisted. The sins listed here may have been signature sins of the Colossian Christians, or they may have simply been the first sins that came to Paul's mind as he rattled off the beginning of a list.

Anger and **rage** are often linked in biblical texts (for example, Rom. 2:8; Eph. 4:31). Most of us know people who have an anger problem, and we know how destructive it can be. Sometimes it is explosive and results in harsh language or actions. Road rage, noisy fights, and physical abuse such as hitting come to

3. Some early manuscripts of Colossians add "on those who are disobedient," which other early manuscripts lack.
4. See also Rom. 11:30; 1 Cor. 6:11; Eph. 2:2; Titus 3:3; 1 Pet. 4:3.

Vice and Virtue Lists

Writers in the ancient Mediterranean world often compiled lists that grouped together a selection of inappropriate behaviors or *vices* as well as a selection of appropriate behaviors or *virtues*.[a] The whole point is to direct people toward the virtues and away from the vices so that they actually live in this way (as opposed to just thinking about the virtues).

One key is the recognition of when something is a vice. A vice is not a onetime action, a blip. A vice is a pattern or lifestyle, an action done again and again, over and over. Craving for inappropriate sex or money or gossip exploits our human weaknesses. We give in to these cravings, engaging again and again in sin. For many of us there is a "signature sin" or two—areas in which we have greater weaknesses. Paul assumes that because non-Christians live only in the present age of sin and brokenness, they give themselves over to these sins and embrace them as lifestyles.

Paul always argues that for Christians the reality is different now, or at least a different reality is possible now. The age to come, also called the kingdom of God, has been inaugurated through Jesus, which means that followers of Jesus have died to sin (with Christ). The new life of freedom from sin is now both a possibility and a goal (see also the sidebar "Defining the Gospel" at Col. 1:5). In other words, lists like this do not give us permission to be passive, as if we could say, "Well, even as Christians we are still sinners, but we don't need to worry about that because of grace." No, the *possibility and goal* is new life in Christ; his resurrection has enabled a life of new creation, of life after death. But this requires *Spirit-empowered effort*; putting sin to death in our lives is an ongoing process of discipleship. This also means that focusing on questions such as "Where is the line? When does something actually become not just an occasional behavior but a vice?" and using the distinction to downplay "occasional" sins misses the point. God's desire for us is not that we attempt to get as close to the line as possible without actually crossing it (everyone I know who has had an extramarital affair, for example, used this argument). Rather, God's desire for us is that we avoid the line altogether. We stay as far away as possible. To use Paul's language, we run away from it (1 Cor. 6:18)!

a. See also Rom. 1:24–32; 12:1–13; 1 Cor. 5:9–11; 6:9–11; Gal. 5:13–6:10; Eph. 4:17–5:20; 1 Thess. 4:1–12; Heb. 13:1–17; 1 Pet. 1:13–4:11.

mind. Sometimes anger simmers, however, and leaks out like steam from the side of a boiling pot with a lid on it. The sarcastic comment, offered at someone else's expense, can be very hurtful. The withdrawal into silence can also be a form of anger, with only a rude glance or even the avoidance of eye contact along with rigid body language as the sign. Often we focus on the results of anger: the unkind word, the slap, the punching of a wall. True discipleship, however, asks about the cause of anger. Why is someone angry? Is there betrayal or injustice? Or is it simply selfishness, the desire to get one's own way? Either way, the Bible is clear that a lifestyle of anger, of rage, is not the way of Jesus. The angry person must be discipled; the energy behind it can and should be directed toward better pursuits that can include working toward justice, repairing relationships, and loving others well.

Next in the list is **malice**. Malice has to do with one's attitude and can also be described as being mean-spirited or vicious.[5] The following three sins on Paul's list are all sins of the tongue: **slander**, **filthy language**, and to **lie** (3:8–9; see also James 1:26). Of course, we all know how destructive such sins can be, and for many of us our "signature sin" is one or a combination of these. Slander is disrespectful speech. For many ancient Mediterranean people, slander was used in public settings such as marketplaces. The point was to shame, to dishonor, by destroying reputations (and what follows from that, including livelihoods). Whether or not we slander today in an open-air market or on social media, the disrespectful speech of many Christians is a sin. It is one thing to disagree; it is quite another thing to be disrespectful in our disagreements. How often is slander combined with malice, a mean-spirited attitude that takes the potshot at someone who appears to be an opponent rather than engaging in a respectful conversation?

Filthy language is language that is in poor taste, is obscene or dirty (including sexually). We all know what filthy language is in our contexts, even if it may vary a bit in flavor from context to context. At the very least this includes swear words and sexual jokes, but if we took seriously all language that is *in poor taste* and set the standard for poor taste at a biblical level, what else would be included? When I was growing up, my mom did not like me to use even the word "sucks." She always called it a dirty word. Does that qualify as filthy language? Perhaps it is not obscene, but does it demonstrate poor taste? Now I have kids of my own, and I encourage them to be more creative (and appropriate) in their use of language compared to many of their peers. Much of the "filthy language" in our context actually requires little effort to use and ends up as a kind of low-bar status quo. I tell my kids that using the default cultural option of a swear word

5. Danker, *Greek-English Lexicon*, s.v. κακία, 443.

or an obscene phrase makes them sound as if they are not very creative. Is that really the best option they could come up with in a moment of frustration or pain? What if, instead of swearing, making an inappropriate joke, or generally speaking in poor taste, we consciously choose to express ourselves more creatively and carefully? What if such language choices open up opportunities for us to share with those around us the reasons why we do not default to the base language of the contexts where we live?

Finally, Paul commands the Colossians, **Do not lie to each other** (3:9). In the ancient Mediterranean world it was considered to be especially inappropriate to lie to people in one's own family or kin group. Paul is assuming that the Colossians, who are brothers and sisters in the Jesus-family, would see the importance of not lying to one another. Lying, as we all know, breaks trust and destabilizes or even destroys relationships. A colleague of mine often says that trust is earned in droplets and lost in buckets. Think about how one lie, once exposed, can derail an entire marriage or friendship. This does not always occur, of course, but it can.

If we really meditate on this vice list, we will feel not just negative conviction but positive direction. In other words, the positive vision is included: if we are not lying to one another, then we are being honest—truthful. If we are not using filthy language, then we are using appropriate, even God-honoring language. If we are not being disrespectful to one another with our words, then we are honoring one another with what we say. An area of tension here is how we consider such vices in our entertainment choices, such as social media, movies, games, books, and music. If I abstain from inappropriate language, should I watch a movie filled with lewd jokes? The Christian saying "Be in the world, but not of it" is connected to what Jesus says in John 17:14–17. What does it mean to be in the world in the arena of entertainment, but not of it? If we hide what we are watching or reading from Christians we respect (our spouses, close friends in our churches, etc.), that is probably a sign that something is amiss. Some people use ratings as a basic guide. Others routinely turn movies off or change the channel or close the book, and a willingness to do so can be part of our ongoing process of discipleship. Asking the question regularly—of whether we are reading, watching, and listening to things that dishonor God—is at least a step in the right direction. Many people are much more discerning regarding what they eat and drink than what they watch. Passages such as Col. 3 remind us to submit our entire lives to Christ's lordship.

After listing all these vices, Paul returns to his larger reason and vision for life in Christ. We should rid ourselves of vices because they are part of the old self: **You have taken off your old self with its practices and have put on the new self, which is being renewed in knowledge in the image of its Creator**

PENTECOSTAL INTEREST

Charles Harrison Mason and the Church of God in Christ

Charles Harrison Mason was born to freed slaves in Tennessee in 1864. He participated in the Azusa Street revival in 1907 and was baptized in the Holy Spirit, speaking in tongues. He describes the experience using the notion of the "old man" (KJV) or "old self" (NIV) that Paul describes in Col. 3:9: "The sound of a mighty wind was in me and my soul cried, 'Jesus, only, one like you.' My soul cried and soon I began to die. It seemed that I heard the groaning of Christ on the cross dying for me. All of the work was in me until I died out of *the old man*. . . . When I opened my mouth to say glory, a flame touched my tongue which ran down to me. My language changed and no word could I speak in my own tongue."[a] Mason later helped to found the Church of God in Christ, the largest pentecostal denomination in the United States.

a. Quoted in Bowens, *African American Readings*, 217 (emphasis hers).

(3:9–10; see also Rom. 6:1–14; Eph. 3:16). The language of "taking off" and "putting on" recalls Paul's comments about circumcision and baptism in Col. 2:11–13 (along with 3:5, 12).

Our old selves have died with Christ, but because the new creation is not fully here yet, the old selves continually try to resurrect themselves. They are like zombies; they appear to be human in some ways but are not fully human. Our old selves are like the old humanity in Genesis who sins; our new selves are like the new humanity in Jesus who participates in new creation. Our new selves will be complete someday when Jesus appears; until that point, we disciples live toward, rather than away from, our future. Someday we will be fully renewed and complete as image bearers of the Creator! Until then, our process of renewal involves our own participation (see also 2 Cor. 4:16).

Paul reminds us here, as he already has in Col. 1:9–10, that such renewal involves **knowledge**.[6] We must know what is true; we must know who and how God has created us so that we can walk, through the power of the Spirit, toward that reality rather than toward what the world offers us (see also Rom. 12:2; Eph. 4:23). In God's image-renewing project distinctions between humans lose

6. Note that in Gen. 3 the forbidden tree is connected to *knowledge*.

their power to separate us, because what unites us is our shared identity as God's image bearers. In Christ we are not **Gentile or Jew, circumcised or uncircumcised, barbarian, Scythian, slave or free** (3:11; see also Gal. 3:28). Of course, people in the first century and today still are Jewish or gentile, circumcised or uncircumcised, though the Colossian church seems to be predominantly gentile. In our churches today we are still often divided by ethnic and/or racial boundaries as well. We have taken it further than many churches in the first century, as we are often not just divided but segregated. Much of the internal conflict in the churches in the New Testament stemmed from their being mixed Jew-gentile communities; they were still together, even though it was challenging. Some churches today have largely given up on this vision of the church, though others are actively embracing (in a variety of ways) this vision for God's people. Spirit of God, empower us in our local contexts to be your people across our ethnic and racial differences, to join together what is so often separated!

Paul also mentions **barbarian** and **Scythian** (3:11). The Greek word *barbaros* was used to described people who were unaware of Greek (or Roman) language and culture; they were seen as uncivilized. The Greek word *Skythēs* was used in a similar way; though technically the region of Scythia was near the Black Sea, the area was stereotypically viewed as ignorant, marginal, and even "savage," on the distant edge of the Roman Empire. Many conquered barbarians and Scythians would have ended up as slaves. Paul here is showing his awareness of these categories as ways that people separate themselves: into groups that are higher (non-barbarian, thus fully part of the Greek culture of the day) or lower (barbarians and Scythians, thus ignorant of "good" culture and appropriate cultural actions). We have our own versions today of who is "cultured" and who is not, of course. Whoever is demeaned by being considered ignorant according to dominant cultural stereotypes is today's "barbarian." In some contexts it may be those from a certain geographical area or from rural areas, those who are "blue collar" or "working class," those who don't speak the dominant language (like English), those without a certain level of education, and so forth. Cultural elites often disrespect these categories of people even while claiming to help them or at least to have the desire to help them. Such help often takes the form of enculturation, of attempting to get today's "barbarians" and "Scythians" to understand and value the dominant or elitist culture. Paul's point here, of course, is that such unjust use of these distinctions is not part of God's image-renewing project. Christians are called to resist boundary making that stratifies people, placing them higher or lower on a ladder of value. Separating people out as either "barbarians" or not, as either culturally elite or not, is not our future.

After mentioning gentiles and Jews, circumcised and uncircumcised, barbarians and Scythians, Paul adds the categories of **slave** and **free** (3:11; see also

1 Cor. 12:13; Gal. 3:28). As discussed in some detail in the introduction (see comments there), the institution of slavery was simply an everyday part of the ancient Mediterranean world. It was one way that people ranked themselves socially, but here Paul states clearly, confidently, that those who bear God's image and are being renewed in that image include both slave and free. For those who are in Christ, who **is all, and is in all** (v. 11; see also Eph. 1:23), those distinctions have been overlaid by a creational reality. Christ, as the one who began both creation and new creation (Col. 1:15–20), offers a much more powerful reality that sees

PENTECOSTAL INTEREST

Pentecostals, Race, and Modern "Barbarians"

Pentecostal history provides a powerful and convicting example of stratification based on racial and cultural elitism. Although the early modern pentecostal movement in the United States, associated with places like Azusa Street in Los Angeles, California, and figures such as William Seymour and Charles Parham, was famously multiracial (and was often ridiculed in the media for that camaraderie), the movement then largely divided itself along ethnic and/or racial lines. The most famous examples are the Church of God in Christ, which was predominantly Black, and the Assemblies of God, which was white. The Spirit's outpouring in the early years of the twentieth century initiated a multiracial community in the United States, but within a couple of decades human organization had stifled it. Many pentecostal communities today are attempting to reembrace their roots, but the reconciliation is slow. The process of being renewed in the image of our Creator is ongoing and unfinished.

The same is true regarding notions of who is a "barbarian" and who is not, who is culturally elite and who is not. Many early pentecostals perceived that they were socially marginalized. "Dregs. Misfits. Drifters. From the beginning outsiders depicted pentecostals largely in such terms."[a] I have been in Spirit-filled contexts today that also understand themselves to be marginalized, and a common response is to stress the "superior" experience of the Holy Spirit, poured out on the in-group in ways that many others—including other Christians—have not experienced. This strategic move makes others in the church the ignorant ones, the "barbarians." Needless to say, both of these understandings of marginal "barbarians" are deeply sinful.

a. Wacker, *Heaven Below*, 199.

the image of God, rather than one's status as slave or free, as primary. Our world today has its own versions of slavery, including human trafficking, and this text denounces those forms of human sin. Even more foundational, however, is Paul's insistence here that the one who is all and in all—Christ, the best of everything—determines who has value, who is worthy of bearing the image of the Creator. Slaves are worthy; the culturally "ignorant" are worthy; the groups deemed racially inferior by other groups are worthy. *Humanity* is worthy, and those "in Christ" are together the human group who can actually embody and live out their true identity as images of the Creator. They are the ones being renewed; they are the ones who are reconciled (1:20). That is our future.

This point may seem fairly obvious to many of us in the twenty-first century. In Paul's first-century world, however, this declaration would have sounded incredibly radical. What would make this radical today is the church actually living this truth. What a powerful witness this would be to a watching world. Attempting to force people to live into this truth is a nonstarter; what we need are the apostles, prophets, pastors, and teachers among us to cast a vision for this kind of life together. It needs to be embraced voluntarily and embodied on a local level, where everyday followers of Jesus do life together, where church really is Jesus-family. In local contexts we take care of one another's kids, share meals and homes, fix one another's toilets, and know what is really going on in one another's lives. We cannot fix the epidemic of loneliness in the United States, but we can make sure that no one in our church, or on our block, is lonely. We cannot repair all the broken families in the world, but we can be a family for people here, in our community, who need a family. We cannot mend the hunger problem on our own, but we can ensure that no one here in our local spaces is hungry. We cannot solve the problems with addiction for everyone, but we can support and love those next to us who are attempting to die to their bondage to food, to alcohol, to social media, or to gambling as an ongoing part of their discipleship. We cannot correct on our own the polarization and disrespectful treatment that we see so prominently in our culture, but we can commit to being a local Jesus-family that resists the dehumanization of such actions; we can speak truth with respect and choose to have the challenging conversations face-to-face, as well as agree to let other things go. It will be difficult. We will make mistakes and hurt one another, but we will commit to practicing forgiveness. We will not hold these offenses against one another. We can do this because the gospel insists on it. And we can do it through the power of the Spirit across ethnic and racial lines and economic divisions, with varying levels of education and exposure, because that is what being "in Christ" means. That is who God's image-renewing project calls us to be. Together.

Participation in this project is not easy, and Paul knows that. His next step is to give us instructions for how to live in this way, as part of God's image-renewing human family: **Therefore, as God's chosen people, holy and dearly loved, clothe yourselves with compassion, kindness, humility, gentleness and patience** (3:12). Paul begins by saying **therefore**, indicating that what he says next is based on what he just said. What he just said is the foundation, which includes especially verses 1–11. He reminds us again who we are—**God's chosen people, holy and dearly loved**—and tells us how our identity shapes what we do and how we live. The image Paul uses is that of clothing. We take clothes off and put them on. Discarding ripped, dirty, or inappropriate clothes is a relief; new clothes are refreshing (see also Rom. 13:14). We also know instinctively that clothes communicate something about us. When we wear something new, it is a statement. People notice. Usually, we feel good in the new article of clothing. When we take on a new role, or a new job, we often adopt a new look, perhaps a uniform or medical scrubs or business attire. We know that we are communicating something about ourselves, our position, our status, and our responsibilities through that clothing.

The first specific item that Paul tells us to wear is **compassion**. The Greek text uses two words here, not one. The second is a word for "compassion" (*oiktirmos*), but the first is the noun *splanchnon*, which can be used literally to designate human entrails and metaphorically to speak of the seat and source of key commitments (such as compassion). In other words, committing to compassion deeply (in our gut, as it were) is the point.[7] I find it quite telling that Paul begins in this way, by telling us to be concerned about others and their troubles. In other words, he is reminding us to focus not on ourselves but on others. Paul uses the word for "compassion" (*oiktirmos*) elsewhere, including for the way in which God cares about us (see, for example, Rom. 12:1; 2 Cor. 1:3; Phil. 2:1). Some Christians seem to be more naturally compassionate; perhaps it is connected to a spiritual gift. For the rest of us, however, compassion is a trait that we must intentionally put on and wear; we must ask the Spirit of God to lead us in compassion.

The next virtue Paul mentions is **kindness**, which has to do with helpfulness and generosity (also mentioned in 2 Cor. 6:6, of him and Timothy, and in Gal. 5:22, as a fruit of the Spirit). Slogans such as "Be kind" are quite popular right now in the United States, with kindness being seen as an ultimate virtue in a diverse society. There is some truth to this, though I often wonder what people mean when they use the word. Helpfulness and generosity can be verbal, in a

---

7. The word *splanchnon* also occurs in Luke 1:78; Acts 1:18; 2 Cor. 6:12; 7:15; Phil. 1:8; 2:1; Philem. 7, 12, 20; 1 John 3:17.

sense; we can allow others to speak, and we can affirm with our own words. But greater kindness will require more from us than simply words, especially if we are to exhibit the kindness that God exhibits toward us (for example, Rom. 2:4; 11:22; Titus 3:4). In other words, if our understanding of kindness is shaped by God's kindness, it has a goal: repentance and redemption. The kindness of secular society appears quite empty next to the fullness of God's reality.

After listing compassion and kindness, Paul includes **humility**. Unlike many contexts today, which value (or say they value) humility, Paul's world typically did not see humility as a virtue. Humility has to do with lowering oneself, with taking steps that intentionally place others above oneself, as Paul says (using the same word) in Phil. 2:3. At least one reason why ancient Mediterranean people were opposed to humility was their culture's clearly defined social stratification. People were ranked on a status ladder according to a host of factors, including family, economics, and whether they were slave or free, and the culture encouraged people to be satisfied with their status or rank. Climbing up the ladder, as is common in many contexts today, was not necessarily a social value in Paul's day. The same was true for descending, however. Why would anyone do that? The answer is Jesus, as this is what Jesus both teaches (Matt. 23:12) and does for us (for example, Phil. 2:5–11). Paul lives and teaches it as well, following Jesus (Acts 20:19; Eph. 4:2; 5:21; see also 1 Pet. 5:5, quoting Prov. 3:34). Paul is aware that humility can be fake and inappropriate, as he has already mentioned in Colossians (2:18, 23); this is one of the problems of the false teachers.

If all Christians in a local community live this way, humbly lowering themselves to place others higher, then everyone will be treated well, and this, of course, is the overall goal. This is not a gift of the few, who then place themselves lower and lower while others take advantage of being higher. No, the goal is a mutual, communal self-lowering, a choice to live like Jesus and so honor other people. Ironically, though contexts like the United States claim to value humility, there is a culture of blatant bragging as well. This comes through obviously in sports, in academic settings, and on social media. My sister calls people "social media braggers" if they post only the beautiful pictures and moments from their lives. This is not an intentional self-lowering; this is an intentional self-raising, and usually at least part of the point is to make others envious. In other words, instead of prioritizing others, we prioritize ourselves, which is not the recipe for healthy community.[8] Social media can be handled well, or at

---

8. Of course, the opposite problem may be the case at times. Instead of bragging, some primarily use social media to complain or make negative comments. This can also be unhealthy if taken to extremes and, paradoxically, can be another form of self-promotion rather than a true exercise in humility.

least more healthily, but our motivations and reactions to others need ongoing discernment as part of our discipleship.

Paul closes out Col. 3:12 with two more virtues: **gentleness** and **patience**. Gentleness is the quality of not being overly impressed by one's self-importance, and the Greek word *prautēs* that Paul uses here can be translated as "humility."[9] He uses it of Christ in 2 Cor. 10:1 and of other Christians in other virtue lists or instructions.[10] It is enjoyable to be around people who possess this trait; a person who is not impressed by herself but directs her celebration and encouragement toward others is someone we want as a friend. And even if she will not be a best friend, she is the kind of person we want in our churches, our Jesus-family. She is living the way of Jesus.

The same is true for patient people; we need them in our lives to show us how to live appropriately as Christians in a messy world. Paul has already used the word "patience" in Col. 1:11, though it's probably most helpful first to think about what patience means when Paul and other New Testament writers talk about God the Father or Jesus (for example, Rom. 2:4; 1 Tim. 1:16; 1 Pet. 3:20; 2 Pet. 3:15). When humans have been incredibly unfaithful and provoked our Creator, how does the Creator respond? With patience. Those of us who have spent time around kids know that kids definitely have their moments of provocation. They resist our guidance; they rebel; they treat one another poorly; they act selfishly. How do we respond? How would God respond? Patience does not mean that there is only grace, of course. Judgment is often part of God's response as well, though it is helpful to remember (as above, with kindness) what the *goal* of patience is: repentance, salvation, restoration. How do we hold on, endure the challenges that others create for us, and keep the big picture of restoration in mind as we live together in Jesus-community? Paul encourages patience in multiple texts,[11] giving us many reminders to practice this virtue. And perhaps that is part of the way that we clothe ourselves with patience. In this in-between time, where we have died with Christ and are raised to life but do not yet fully experience (bodily) resurrection life, we keep dressing ourselves in patience. We put it on again and again, partly because we keep taking it off accidentally or forgetfully. We do life with a community of people who remind us to put it back on. We read Scripture and are reminded again. We pray that the Spirit will empower us to live with patience,[12] with endurance, as we await our future.

---

9. Danker, *Greek-English Lexicon*, s.v. πραΰτης, 764.

10. For example, Gal. 5:23; Eph. 4:2; 2 Tim. 2:25; Titus 3:2. For its use in other New Testament texts not authored by Paul, see James 1:21; 3:13; 1 Pet. 3:16.

11. For example, 2 Cor. 6:6; Gal. 5:22; Eph. 4:2; 2 Tim. 3:10; 4:2. See also Heb. 6:12; James 5:10.

12. Paul says directly in texts such as Gal. 5:22 that virtues such as patience are fruits of the Spirit; they are not traits that we can acquire and live out in our own human power.

Paul is a realist. He knows that living in community is hard; he has experienced it. In Ephesus, a city not far from Colossae, Paul spent a total of about three years. In Corinth, across the Aegean Sea, he lived for about eighteen months. In other words, in these two locations Paul stayed long enough to do real community with people. Enough time had passed that the shininess, the "honeymoon stage," of church had ended. Beyond this, Paul also has some long-term coworkers, people like Silas, Timothy, and Priscilla. When we are in honest human relationships that last, we sometimes (or often!) hurt one another, and Paul knows this.

The way to maintain the relationship is not to ignore these hurts but rather to move through them—to forgive. Colossians 3:13 teaches this: **Bear with each other and forgive one another if any of you has a grievance against someone. Forgive as the Lord forgave you** (see also Eph. 4:2, 32). This is directly connected to the command in the previous verse to **clothe yourselves with . . . patience** (3:12). This is real life. This is also not optional; it is part of what it means to follow Jesus and be his disciple. He forgives; we forgive. Jesus makes a very similar point in Matt. 6:9–13 when he teaches his disciples to pray. Part of the Lord's Prayer is to urgently, desperately ask God to forgive us *as we forgive* (v. 12). God's forgiveness and ours are linked. Jesus makes this even clearer two verses later when he says, "For if you forgive other people when they sin against you, your heavenly Father will also forgive you. But if you do not forgive others their sins, your Father will not forgive your sins" (vv. 14–15). This is Jesus talking here, and he is trustworthy and authoritative. God's forgiveness of us is connected to our forgiveness of others; we can *exclude ourselves* from God's forgiveness if we do not forgive others.

I have often heard people ask good, fair questions at this point. What does forgiveness actually look like? What about people who do not deserve to be forgiven? I reply that the end goal of forgiveness is always the same: repentance, salvation, restoration, reconciliation. However, we cannot control the other person's or party's response. Full reconciliation involves the participation of at least two people or groups, and if one withholds or refuses to engage, then it is not possible. However, even if the end goal is not met, forgiveness can still achieve a partial goal. Forgiveness is about release: letting go of the wrong rather than holding it tightly and closely.

In my fallen self I am a grudge holder. I am terrible at forgiving. My tendency is to hold the wrong not just closely but (metaphorically) at eye level. I like to look at it often, to remind myself of how that person or group has hurt me. I tell myself how terrible they are, how they do not deserve to be forgiven—at least not in a generous way. If I do forgive them, my sinful self wants to forgive them only as far or as much as they deserve, which is only a tiny amount. But here is the thing: that is not the way God forgives us (for example, Ps. 103:10–12; Luke 23:34). If God forgives us only as much or as far as we deserve, we are in trouble. God forgives abundantly, overwhelmingly, and we are called to this kind of forgiveness as well: to release the wrong in a big "whoosh" like a stiff breeze, to release it the way a frisbee is set free when it flies through the air.

When I am in the process of forgiving (and it is often a process for me, not a moment), I will say out loud, "I am forgiving this person. I am. I still am. Spirit of God, help me to forgive, to keep forgiving." And in this way I participate in my own freedom rather than my binding. I know several people who are locked up in unforgiveness. They have been deeply, legitimately hurt, and they will not forgive; they will not release it. And that clenching has birthed a hardness in them; it is as if their bitterness has grown up and around them until it surrounds their entire selves. They have participated in their own imprisonment. What I have noticed is that this has destroyed their lives in many ways, including making it hard for them to develop and maintain healthy relationships.[13]

The final piece of clothing that we are to wear is **love** (3:14). This is because of what love is able to do: bind the other virtues **together in perfect unity** (v. 14). Paul has already talked about love in this letter (1:4, 8; 2:2; 3:12). Love is a favorite topic of his, and it appears in many other New Testament books as well.[14] Many ancient Jews, Greeks, and Romans also valued love as a virtue, but in Christian literature it is the supreme virtue, likely following the priority Jesus placed on it (for example, Matt. 22:36–40). It is worth noting again that in the Bible love is not seen primarily as a feeling or emotion but rather is connected to commitment and sacrifice. It also has a goal in that it moves us closer to who God designed us to be as humans made in God's image. This is how God loves us, of course. This also means that we can love people that we do not like, because we can still be committed to them and sacrifice for them. Or perhaps I should say that our commitment to them encourages us to be compassionate, kind, humble, gentle, patient, and forgiving (Col. 3:12–13).

Paul's most famous discussion of love is in 1 Cor. 13:1–13, often called the "love chapter" and read at wedding ceremonies. What is sometimes missed is that there Paul is talking about love in Christian community, not love in marriage. In a larger section on spiritual gifts and the abuse of those gifts by members of the Corinthian church, which leads to their abuse of one another (chaps. 12–14), Paul

---

13. Paul here is discussing the interpersonal level of forgiveness *within* Christian community. Sometimes, of course, one group wrongs another group, and forgiveness and reconciliation are more complicated in such situations, though for Christian groups texts such as this can still speak powerfully.

14. For example, Rom. 5:2–5; 13:8–10; 1 Cor. 13:1–13; Gal. 5:5–6; Eph. 4:2–5; 1 Thess. 1:3; 5:8; see also Matt. 22:37–40; Heb. 6:10–12; 1 John 3:11–18; 4:7–5:3.

insists that they love one another. Love will correct their abuses of one another. He concludes this well-known teaching by saying, "And now these three remain: faith, hope and love. But the greatest of these is love" (13:13). Why is love the greatest? Ben Witherington explains, "Because it alone never fails and will in fact carry on into the next life. Faith will become sight and hope will be fulfilled, but love will simply carry on, presumably amplified and purified into a perfect condition. It is the one attribute that is to bridge this age and the eschatological reality."[15] In other words, when new creation is complete and we hug Jesus in our resurrected bodies, love will remain. We will see new creation and Jesus as the initiator of it, and our hope and faith will be fulfilled—satisfied. But love will remain.

How do we clothe ourselves with love above all else? Many ancient writers, including biblical authors, used the image of clothing when talking about vices (disrobe!) and virtues (get dressed!) (see, for example, Job 29:14; Isa. 61:10). If you have ever tried to will yourself to love others, you know how challenging, and even impossible, this is to do in your own power. Our will is simply not strong enough. But Paul reminds us elsewhere that we have access to a love greater than ourselves because it comes from God and has been given to us through the Holy Spirit (Rom. 5:2–5; Col. 1:8; see also Gal. 5:5–6; Eph. 4:2–5). We have the Spirit! Pentecostals and charismatics, we who regularly affirm and walk with the Spirit, practicing our spiritual gifts and relying on the Spirit's empowerment, should be the most loving people around. If we are not, perhaps this can be a focus of our discipleship starting now. What might the Spirit do in us and through us if we rely on him to help us love others? If we ask him to help us love in deeper and bigger ways? If we did not try to love others in our own power and then give up when it does not work well? What if we actually embodied what Paul teaches in 1 Cor. 14:1: "Follow the way of love"? If we do, we will end up where Paul wishes us to end and "do everything in love" (1 Cor. 16:14).

The **peace** that only **Christ** can give must **rule in** our **hearts** (Col. 3:15). Paul has already mentioned peace in this letter, in the greeting: "Grace and peace to you from God our Father" (1:2). Here peace is, as is typical in Paul's letters, connected to what Christ has accomplished. Christ is the one who offers it (1:20; see also John 14:27). Peace includes both personal or individual peace with God (as reconciliation) and the larger dimensions of interpersonal and even communal/corporate harmony, as in the Hebrew understanding of *shalom* (see also Num. 6:24–26). This communal focus is what Paul is stressing here in Col. 3:15, as the rest of the verse makes clear: **Since as members of one body you**

---

15. Witherington, *Conflict and Community*, 272. Some scholars argue that faith, hope, and love will all remain as eschatological realities. This is possible, though in Rom. 8:24 and 2 Cor. 5:7 Paul seems to say otherwise. Or perhaps Paul is working with slightly different definitions of "hope" and "faith" in each text.

were called to peace. We are called to it, as we are called as God's people (beginning with Abraham in Gen. 12:1–3). This kind of harmony, of reconciliation in relationships, is something that we must do (see also Rom. 14:19). In Col. 3:15 the call to *let* peace rule is, in the Greek text, an imperative, a command: peace *must* rule. It must be the arbiter or umpire for our life together in community.

Christ's reconciling power should have control over the core of who we are physically, spiritually, and mentally—all of it. If this is true in our lives, we will forgive as Christ did (Col. 3:13). We will prioritize others over ourselves (v. 12). We will embody the kind of community we were created to be, the healthy, appropriately interdependent body of Christ, where all belong and have significant parts to play, and we will do so in and through the power of the Holy Spirit (3:15; see also 1:18; 2:19; Rom. 12:5; 1 Cor. 12:12–27; Eph. 4:3–4). I am struck by the force of this language. We are commanded to live in this way. It is not an option; it is not what we can take up if we feel like it. We *must*. Our communities must look more and more like this picture, or we are missing the point of texts like these and endangering our own discipleship. This could be applied more broadly, to Christians in general, but here Paul is talking about the local church. Would you use Paul's language here to describe your local community of Jesus followers? Are you as a group growing in your discipleship and maturity in this way, where Christ's reconciling force unites you ever more deeply, even if sometimes you act selfishly? Even with that person who really annoys you? Even when (not if, but when) someone hurts you? Are we able to be thankful in and through this process, as Paul adds here (Col. 3:15) but also mentions in many other texts?[16] The sense is of *ongoing* thankfulness; we should be thankful people generally. Are you known as a thankful, grateful person? Is your church known to be so?

I have a friend who is a professor of education, and her research focuses on gratitude. Basically, her research is affirming what the Bible has been teaching all along. When we do not remind ourselves of what is good in our lives, when we do not express gratitude for God's gifts to us, we tend to default to negativity. In other words, most of us need to be intentional about recognizing our blessings. What if a "gratitude practice" became a part of our ongoing discipleship, not just individually but as a church? What if we told others—even people who annoy us or have hurt us in the past—that we are grateful that God put them in our lives? What might the Spirit unleash in our communities if we became known as thankful people, even in pain, even in economic hardship, even in uncertainty?

This will be easier if we take Paul's next command seriously: **Let the message of Christ dwell among you richly** (3:16; see "dwell" also in 1:19). This

---

16. See also Rom. 7:25; 1 Cor. 14:18; Phil. 1:3; Col. 1:3, 12; Philem. 4.

verse has a strong parallel in Eph. 5:18–19, which emphasizes the Spirit. Here in Colossians Paul emphasizes Christ (though he also mentions the Spirit). This difference is likely due to the specific issue in the Colossian church where false teachers were limiting the scope of Christ's role. That this is a command means, again, that it *must* be the case. It is not optional. The **message of Christ** probably is a shorthand reference for knowing and remembering both the human and the divine natures of Christ. This includes his role as the preexistent Son, who creates and holds all things together (Col. 1:15–20), as well as his earthly life (including his teachings and miracles), death, resurrection, ascension, and pouring out of the Spirit. All of this is connected deeply to the Old Testament promises of God's restoration for God's people and the broader creation, which Jesus has now inaugurated (see also Rom. 10:17). In other words, we must be grounded in this truth; it must dwell among us (us, not me!—the Greek is plural) in a rich, decadent, pervasive way. These biblical stories must be our stories, deeply familiar and powerful in how they shape the way that we understand ourselves and the world. My husband is a teacher and a natural storyteller. One of the ways that he serves in our local church is as a teacher in the elementary kids' ministry. He tells the Bible stories and is known for connecting a smaller story to the big story of the whole Bible. He tells the kids, again and again, that everything goes back to Gen. 1–3. God's plan through Israel, Jesus, and the church is to bring the world back to (renewed) creation, to walking with God in the cool of the day. And kids remember it.

If this Christ-message actually does dwell among us as a community (again, the Greek word for "you" in Col. 3:16 is plural), we will be able to **teach and admonish one another with all wisdom**. In other words, teaching and admonishing will be the task not just of a few leaders but of the entire community. Significantly, in Col. 1:28 Paul says that he and Timothy are "teaching" and "admonishing"—the same Greek words! The task is not just theirs, however; all Christians are equipped to teach and admonish. An academic mentor of mine has told me many times that if he had to choose a favorite passage in Scripture, it would be Col. 3:16. The beauty of this text that is so communal and mutual moves him deeply. If all in our local churches were deeply steeped in Scripture because they had soaked in it, retelling and rereading the stories again and again, what wisdom might that offer us? Might we be better equipped to teach and admonish? Admonishing is *warning*; we should be able to warn *one another* about behaviors and attitudes that are not aligned with the life of new creation. This might seem impossible to do in some of our contexts for a variety of reasons, including the reality that many Christians do not know their Bibles very well. Fewer people now actually read and reread their Bibles, soaking in Scripture and even memorizing passages. How many people in our churches do not know the Bible well? How many have read even a few books in their entirety, let alone the entire Bible?

A second reason why it might be challenging for us to teach and warn one another has to do with the current cultural idea that we are all basically decent people: everyone is fine, everyone is a good person. At least, this is what a lot of current culture tells us (though even here there are major exceptions for groups that are out of dominant social favor, such as sexual assaulters, who clearly are *not* fine). The Bible, of course, does not hold this view. It agrees that humans were created good (Gen. 1:31), but it also insists that humans, following Adam and Eve, are fallen (Gen. 3:6; Rom. 3:23). We are both: good and sinful, fine and not fine. However, if we in the church buy into this cultural idea that everyone is fine as they are, it will be difficult to teach and warn one another. We might wonder if warning another Christian is appropriate, and sometimes it may not be. There are factors to consider: Do we know them very well? How are they living? How confident are we in the Spirit's direction? Is our motivation to judge and find fault, or is it to seek the goal of repentance and restoration? Paul and Timothy's end goal for teaching and warning is "so that we may present everyone fully mature in Christ" (Col. 1:28). Is that our goal as well? For these reasons, and others, many of us simply avoid texts like Col. 3:16 and never warn anyone. In Spirit-filled contexts, where we insist that the Spirit is poured out on and empowers all of us, it is surprising that texts like Col. 3:16 do not get more attention. We are empowered by the Spirit to teach and warn one another, provided we are steeped in Scripture and attuned to the Spirit's leading.

We are also to sing **psalms, hymns, and songs from the Spirit, singing to God with gratitude** (3:16; compare Eph. 5:19).[17] In the Old Testament the psalms make up Israel's songbook, of course. At least some of them were sung as the people of God gathered and celebrated a variety of festivals and other events (see especially Ps. 47:7). The word for "hymn" (*hymnos*) was used in the ancient Mediterranean world of songs sung to deities or heroes. Here, of course, the Lord is the deity in question. Some early Christian hymns might possibly be found in texts such as Phil. 2:6–11 and Col. 1:15–20 (see also Acts 16:25), though it is unclear whether those passages were actually sung or just read. The third item, the songs, is connected to the Spirit, as the adjective *pneumatikos* ("spiritual") is related to the noun *pneuma* ("Spirit"). Some translations read "spiritual songs" here, but the translation **songs from the Spirit** makes the Spirit's presence and agency clearer. For Paul, anything truly "spiritual" is connected to the Holy

---

17. The Greek can be translated in two main ways. The first indicates that we teach and warn *by using* the psalms, hymns, and songs, though this seems to be quite a limited understanding of how teaching and warning occur. The second sees the teaching and warning as the first command, while singing psalms, hymns, and songs is the second command.

Spirit. Such songs may be spontaneous or even glossolalic—that is, sung in tongues (see also 1 Cor. 14:15; Eph. 5:18–19).[18] In many charismatic contexts today spontaneous singing in tongues is a common practice, and passages like this offer biblical support. We insist that the Spirit often surprises us because there is an active, dynamic element to the Spirit's work—in creation broadly, and in us. In other words, the Spirit isn't just hovering over creation and sustaining it in a static way; there is ongoing movement. And we can pray that the Spirit will act in fresh ways, and the Spirit responds! There is a kind of partnership here or, better, a relationship, as relationships are dynamic, not static. Recently one of the worship leaders in our church broke out into a spontaneous song about God's power over anxiety, and this text came to mind. The Spirit was at work in her song.

Also worthy of note is the fact that apparently women are participants in these communal activities (including teaching and warning; compare 1 Cor. 14:26). Because Paul mentions Nympha in Col. 4:15, along with the church in her house, we know that women were full participants in the Christian community in Colossae,[19] as they should be today. In many Spirit-filled contexts women are allowed to lead in singing (including spontaneously and in tongues), though in fewer contexts are women allowed to teach and warn. Perhaps it is time to return to the teaching of this verse and embody the truth of it in our own settings more regularly.

At the end of Col. 3:16 Paul again adds a comment on gratitude: **Singing to God with gratitude in your hearts** (compare the end of v. 15). We should sing with gratitude in our hearts (see also Eph. 5:19–20). The connection between singing and gratitude is telling. How many of us sing out of duty rather than gratitude when we are "in church" with other followers of Jesus? Certain songs encourage gratitude in us; others certainly do not. Sometimes the songs are not well written, either musically or lyrically (or both). Sometimes the content of the lyrics is distracting, especially if it is not good theology and not tied to Scripture. The connection between gratitude and singing can be relevant in personal settings as well, when we are listening to music at work, at home, or while commuting. Some songs actually encourage us to feel envious or angry

---

18. Gordon Fee thinks that spontaneous songs are in view here (*God's Empowering Presence*, 653). He does not support the notion of songs in tongues, but this is connected to his view that the "teaching and warning" earlier in the verse is done through the singing of psalms, hymns, and songs from the Spirit. In other words, he observes that it is difficult for unintelligible words to teach and warn (654n71).

19. Gordon Fee makes this point about Nympha. He adds that some later scribes who copied Colossians changed the female name "Nympha" to the male name "Nymphas" because they were uncomfortable with the idea of a church meeting in a woman's house (*God's Empowering Presence*, 649n57).

or lustful. How often are we listening to and singing those songs—and feeding the core of our physical, spiritual, and mental selves—with sinful attitudes and impulses? And how often do we sing songs that stimulate gratitude, reminding us of who God is and what he has done for us and creation? What is your current favorite song that encourages thankfulness to God along with a desire to see others live in freedom, that encourages you to invite others to die with Christ and be raised (Col. 2:12; 3:1)?

Paul mentions thankfulness one more time in the following verse, indicating again how important this posture is: **And whatever you do, whether in word or deed, do it all in the name of the Lord Jesus, giving thanks to God the Father through him** (3:17; see also 1 Cor. 10:31; Eph. 5:20). This passage is often quoted alone as a kind of Christian slogan, and it may indeed be appropriate as a summary of Christian faith. However, are we losing some of the richness of this text when we do not remind ourselves of what comes before it, especially earlier in Col. 3? There, Paul reminds us of who we are and will be (vv. 1–4) and what this means for what we must and must not do (vv. 5–9, put to death things of an earthly nature; vv. 10–16, live the life of the new self). In other words, doing something in Jesus's name means that it must be pleasing to Jesus; this includes our speech (no filthy language, no lies, etc.) and deeds (how we act sexually, how we treat others, etc.). Perhaps our imaginations can be powerfully sparked by comparing Paul's instructions here to what is typical in his world: "Ancient culture was pervasively religious, but most pagan religious practices were ritual observances that did not cast moral influence over one's daily life and ethics. For Paul, by contrast, every aspect of life must be determined by Christ's lordship."[20] Said differently, the moral choices of the Greco-Roman gods and goddesses typically were not worthy of imitation; the God of the Bible, however, embodied in the person of Jesus, definitely is.

---

20. Keener, *Bible Background Commentary*, 578.

Embodying the Reality (2)

Embodying Christ in the Household

After talking about the challenge and beauty of community life (Col. 3:5–17), Paul narrows his focus specifically to the ancient household in the next section. In other words, Christ's lordship also affects how people live in the household because Christ is Lord over every area of our lives. At least some of this next section of text may have been written to correct the false teaching that overly encouraged mystical experiences that included visions and angels, as well as extreme fasting (2:16–19). In contrast, followers of Jesus should pursue a faithful life in the seemingly mundane experiences of the everyday household.

Very few ancient Mediterranean people lived only with nuclear families. For most, the ancient household included slaves (if the family could afford them), extended family, and even nonrelatives who may have been attached to the household for a variety of reasons, including trade-related business. Also noteworthy is the reality that very few women stayed home all day and managed the children and food as their only task. Only elite, wealthy women would have had that opportunity (though slaves probably would have done most of the child-rearing and food preparation in wealthy families). Most women worked in the family trade or business along with men and would have needed to spend time in the fields (in rural areas) or in the streets and marketplaces (in cities). The household was viewed as the basic public (not private) social and economic unit of life generally and of the Roman Empire specifically. Stable households were good for the empire. An awareness of this reality prepares us to read Paul's instructions well so that we can note the ways in which the ancient context is both similar to and different from ours. This matters even more because the early churches often met in homes (see the comments on Nympha at Col. 4:15). Christians are, after all, brothers and sisters, a new kind of kin group centered on Jesus.

Scholars call this section of Colossians the "household code." It has at least partial parallels in Eph. 5:21–6:9; 1 Tim. 2:8–15; 6:1–2; Titus 2:1–10; 1 Pet. 2:13–3:7. The Greek philosopher Aristotle, living several hundred years before Paul, seems to have created the structure of the household code. He addressed how a husband should manage his wife, his children, and his slaves (*Politics* 1.1253b).[1] Many other thinkers adopted Aristotle's basic model, probably at least partly because the Romans, as the ruling group in Paul's day, often were suspicious of minority religious groups. Affirming Aristotle's household code became a way for these groups to show that they supported the dominant (Greco-Roman) cultural value system and were not a threat to the social order.

In some ways Paul likewise follows Aristotle's format closely here, first addressing wives and husbands, then children and fathers/parents, and finally slaves and masters. However, what are often not recognized are the ways Paul departs from Aristotle's framework. The first is that Paul addresses the wives (and children and slaves) directly; he talks to them, rather than about them, unlike Aristotle. Also, he addresses the wives (and children and slaves) first; the husbands are addressed second. We would say today that Paul treats the wives as if they have agency; they can choose how to respond to their husbands. Paul tells them, **Submit yourselves to your husbands, as is fitting in the Lord** (3:18). Wives were expected to submit to husbands in the ancient world. This was the status quo, and some readers today, both Christian and not, see Paul as simply affirming the cultural norm. Non-Christians tend to critique this as abusive patriarchy, whereas some Christians see Paul teaching that, in this case, the world's standards are the same as God's standards.

What is worth noting is how in chapter 3 Paul has most recently been addressing how Christians are to treat one another. When he commands us to teach and warn one another (v. 16), to love (v. 14), and to clothe ourselves with virtues that help us defer to others rather than our own selfish desires (v. 12), the model in those verses is mutual submission. In other words, if submission is about prioritizing or deferring to the other over oneself, then Paul has already been teaching that truth, and that truth applies to husbands as well as wives if both are part of the church. Notice that Paul does not tell wives to obey but rather to **submit** (*hypotassō*), a word that stresses the notion of order and is used

---

1. Among Greek-speaking Jewish writers, see Josephus, *Against Apion* 2.201–17. For more discussion see Keener, *Paul, Women and Wives*, chap. 4.

in military texts. Paul employs it in regard not just to marriage (Eph. 5:21–22; Titus 2:5; see also 1 Pet. 3:1)[2] but also to governmental authorities (Rom. 13:1, 5; Titus 3:1; see also 1 Pet. 2:13), to how the church and "everything" submit to Christ and Christ to the Father (1 Cor. 15:27–28; Eph. 5:24; see also James 4:7), and to how Christians treat one another in community more generally (1 Cor. 16:16; Eph. 5:21; see also 1 Cor. 14:32; 1 Pet. 5:5; compare Gal. 5:13). In other words, the emphasis here is on *order* and on the woman choosing to contribute to order rather than chaos in the household.

There are three main options for how to understand this text. The first is that this command to submit is not connected to other problems in the letter: women should submit to husbands simply because the Lord commands it, and in this case the Lord's command matches the status quo of the culture. The woman self-orders under her husband. The second option is that there could be a specific problem in this church that needs to be addressed: perhaps some wives have been influenced by the false teaching that is infiltrating this church (see Col. 2:4, 8, 16–23), and they need to submit and thus contribute to order as they are taught solid teaching. This view typically argues that Paul is also carefully subverting traditional notions of authority in the household. The third option falls between the first two: this text shows Paul's familiarity with Roman concerns over "eastern cults" that subvert conventional Roman family values, and (as Colossae is in the eastern part of the Roman Empire) Paul is careful here to guide the church so that they do not create unnecessary problems in their local contexts. This third option may see Paul affirming the basic status quo (along with the first option) or see Paul working to subvert the status quo in careful ways.

Paul modifies the household code again when he tells wives to submit **as is fitting** [anēkō] **in the Lord** (3:18). The Lord is given here as part of the rationale or description. In other words, we again have two options for how to understand this language. The first is that women should submit to husbands because the Lord requires it; it is in that way fitting. The second is that they should submit in a way that makes sense in Jesus and is shaped by his life, death, and resurrection; this would be a more specific understanding of submission, expressed in the translation "to the degree that is fitting in the Lord."[3] In other words, submission in Christ means that it must be appropriate and fitting and not a copy of the way the world sees submission. This would parallel the way that Paul asks Philemon to do what is "fitting" (also *anēkō*) in Philem. 8 (see comments there): Philemon must receive Onesimus

2. The word is used also for Jesus's submission to his parents in Luke 2:51 and for slaves in Titus 2:9; 1 Pet. 2:18.
3. Dunn, *Epistles*, 248.

as a brother, not as a slave. Because what is "fitting" in Philemon is so deeply countercultural, what is "fitting" in Colossians (a letter written to people in the same church in Colossae) would be countercultural as well. As N. T. Wright argues, "It is, in fact, extremely unlikely that Paul, having warned the young Christians against conforming their lives to the present world, would now require just that of them after all."[4] In other words, such submission cannot include worldly notions of superiority, power, and status (and also obviously cannot be abusive), as Jesus redefines such notions. The specific shape of this in both Paul's world and ours can vary and requires discernment. This may seem mundane in many contexts today, but to give such agency to ancient wives (to self-submit or self-order, as it were, in ways that make sense in the Lord) would have been fairly radical.

There are some other ancient non-Christian writers who also affirm versions of mutuality in marriage, including Xenophon and Musonius Rufus,[5] but only Paul introduces or frames his household codes with mutual submission (as I already noted above, in his teaching in Col. 3:12–16; the parallel text in Eph. 5:21–6:9 is even more explicit). Paul also talks about the authority that wives and husbands have over each other's bodies, another form of mutual submission, in 1 Cor. 7:1–5. Of course, many others, both Jewish and not, were deeply committed to a form of male leadership that today we would call cruel and abusive. This includes physical beatings and "easy" divorces that could leave a woman with no protection and livelihood (note also Jesus's prohibitions of divorce in the Gospels).[6]

With this in mind, the impact of Paul's instructions to husbands is even more powerful: **Husbands, love your wives and do not be harsh with them** (3:19). The word for "love" is written in a way that stresses ongoing love; the point is for husbands to "keep loving" or "always be loving" to wives. The second aspect here, not being harsh, follows from the first: loving well. In other words, if I love someone well, I obviously cannot be harsh with them. The opposite is not true, however; I can resist being harsh to someone even if I do not love them.

4. Wright, *Colossians and Philemon*, 151.

5. Craig Keener ("Mutual Submission") observes, "Four or five centuries before Paul, Xenophon argues in *Oeconomicus* for partnership (*koinōnia*) between spouses (7.18, 30). Still, Xenophon does not envision complete complementarity; he contends that nature has suited wives' bodies better for indoor work and husbands' for work outdoors (7.22–23, 30). The husband has more courage (7.25), but both are equals in memory and self-control (7.26–27)." He adds that the first-century Stoic thinker Musonius Rufus "viewed women as equal to men in nature and virtues" (citing, for example, Musonius Rufus, 4.10–35; 4.31–37; 4.1–26 [Lutz, "Musonius," 44, 46, 48]). "Although he distinguished their roles, he also often disagreed with the restrictive roles to which his society had limited women" (citing Musonius Rufus, 3.25–28 [Lutz, "Musonius," 40]).

6. See Matt. 5:31–32; 19:3–9; Mark 10:2–12; Luke 16:18.

Love typically was not commanded of husbands in ancient Mediterranean culture, and so this is another addition by Paul to the basic format of the household code. Here Scot McKnight is eminently quotable:

> Love in the Bible is covenantal commitment to presence, advocacy, and flourishing growth into Christlikeness (see Col 1:4, 8, 13; 2:2; 3:12, 14). These four elements can now be said of the husband's love of his wife: (1) love is a covenant commitment to one's wife (2) to be with her, (3) to be for her, including providing for her, and (4) to pursue Christlikeness together (the focus of Christ's love in Eph 5:25–26). That is, the direction is redemptive, and all dimensions of the relationship are shaped by Christlike behavior (Christoformity) aimed at fostering Christlikeness in one another.[7]

McKnight continues,

> Husbands who love like this . . . do not make demands, do not overpower, and do not violate the integrity of a wife. Instead, the husband who loves like this encourages, empowers, and frees. The more emphasis that is given to love in Col 3:19, the less emphasis will be given to discussions about power and male . . . authority in 3:18. . . . The more emphasis given to love, the more Spirit-driven will be the relationship of husband and wife. The text, then, does not advocate sharing power; it advocates sharing life and love with one another as a *new kind of power*.[8]

How might marriage relationships be more Spirit-driven? Might a strong focus on human power and authority (who has it, who does not) actually work to quench the Spirit and desensitize us to the Spirit's leading in our marriages? Isn't the Spirit the one leading the way, rather than either human marriage partner? In contexts like the United States we often focus on rights. Whose right is it? Who deserves what? But an intense focus on our rights can end in selfishness and even idolatry if our highest concern is our own rights rather than God's understanding of who we are individually, in marriage, and in community. In Paul's world only rarely were rights discussed. A much bigger social concern was honor, which is the public recognition of a person's (or community's) status and social standing. Honor has to do not with how we feel about ourselves but with how others view us and where we rank on the ladder of importance. In the household code Paul is not talking about rights; he is challenging the person who has more social honor and power in that ancient context—the man—to use it not for himself but for his wife. Using one's honor on behalf of another, rather than oneself, is a kind of submission. "Some object, 'But submission is

7. McKnight, *Colossians*, 349–50.
8. McKnight, *Colossians*, 350 (emphasis mine).

explicit only for the wife!' Ah, but the command to love is explicit only for the husband. . . . Yet we understand that all Christians should love another . . . and that all Christians should submit to one another ([Eph.] 5:21)."[9] Said differently, if submission is self-ordering oneself under another, the wife should defer to and sacrifice for her husband, consistently putting his needs above her own. But that is also what love is: sacrifice and commitment.

This is messy in real life, of course, and is even messier when only one of the partners is a Christian, which certainly would often have been the case in Colossae (and also happens today). Adding to the mess is the reality that, culturally speaking, the institution of marriage is set up quite differently today in many contexts than it was in the Roman Empire. Most people in the United States choose their own marriage partners and marry in their twenties or thirties. In Paul's world the choice of marriage partners was made primarily by families and communities, not the individuals themselves. People often married much younger, women as early as age twelve and (Jewish) men often at age eighteen or a bit later (though some gentile men often married around age thirty). Notions of "consent" in ancient marriage (and some marriages today) were shaped by communal expectations, not primarily by what each individual decided. Many Christians, in the ancient world and today, have lived in marriages where, because of the unwillingness of one partner or the family or culture, they have been unable to make changes to marriage frameworks and patterns. Often they have chosen to live as faithfully as possible, honoring Christ, in those marriages. The complexity of this reality is why we need the Spirit's help; we need guidance in the mess. How can we follow the Spirit in our marriages, especially if the partners disagree about what that means? How can we take Paul's commands in the household code seriously, even as we acknowledge that some aspects of the household code—such as the section on slaves and masters—are not as directly relevant to us?

The beauty of being Spirit-led, rather than culture-led, is that Christian marriages can and should look different in the United States than they do in Brazil or China or Nigeria. In some contexts the woman may at times be the more "powerful" social partner in a marriage, depending on her job, income, beauty, and so forth. How might she use her status well to serve and support her husband as they follow Christ together? In our own marriage and family my husband and I are attempting to live out a covenantal relationship of mutual support and sacrifice for each other. We both work full-time jobs outside the home, and my husband actually quit a job so that I could take my current

---

9. Keener, "Mutual Submission"; Keener makes this point in regard to Eph. 5:21–6:9, but it is relevant here in Colossians as well.

role, which required a move across the country. We have heard the statistics that even when both husband and wife work outside the home, the wife still usually carries the larger share of domestic responsibilities, and we are working to share those responsibilities and live into a (more and more) mutual partnership. It is messy; things fall through the cracks. We both do laundry, but if one of us does not get to it fast enough, then sometimes there are no clean socks. He does (or oversees the kids doing) most of the cleaning. Sometimes this does not happen often enough for my liking. But if I take charge of it, I create an imbalance in our relationship, as I tend to become resentful at the extra responsibility while also limiting his options to serve our family. We are very intentional about sharing our parenting responsibilities, and as teachers we often have similar schedules. However, my job requires much more work in the summer than his, and this leads to him taking the lead parenting role during those months.

Perhaps the following illustration best sums up our marriage. Several years ago my husband and I were having a discussion, and we could not agree. He looked at me, paused, then said in a joking voice, "Woman, submit!" (see Eph. 5:22). I looked at him, paused, then responded in my own joking voice, "When was the last time you gave up your life for me?" (see Eph. 5:25). Giving up one's life is one of the ways the New Testament defines love (John 15:13), and in that moment we were reminding each other of what we are attempting to do, to be, together, as we sacrifice for each other, support each other, and walk behind Jesus together. Spirit, lead us.

After wives and husbands, Paul addresses children and parents: **Children, obey your parents in everything, for this pleases the Lord** (3:20). As in the commands to wives and husbands, the language may indicate ongoing action, with the sense of "keep obeying" or "always obey." However, whereas wives "submit" (*hypotassō* [v. 18]), children "obey" (*hypakouō* [v. 20]). The obedience is to *parents*, not simply fathers, though fathers had the primary cultural and legal authority over children in Paul's day (though see v. 21).

This word for "obey" is used in the New Testament in a variety of contexts, including texts that discuss obedience to sin or to the gospel/Christ/God[10] and other household codes (Eph. 6:1, 5; 1 Pet. 3:6). Colossians 3:20 states that obedience to parents **pleases the Lord**, but in the parallel text in Ephesians, Paul adds a biblical reason for this obedience, quoting from one of the Ten Commandments: "'Honor your father and mother'—which is the first commandment with a promise—'so that it may go well with you and that you may enjoy

---

10. See, for example, Mark 4:41; 8:25; Luke 8:25; Acts 6:7; Rom. 6:12, 16; 10:16; Phil. 2:12; 2 Thess. 1:8; 3:14; Heb. 11:8.

long life on the earth'" (Eph. 6:1–3; see Exod. 20:12).[11] True obedience is about honor, but honoring is about more than obedience. In other words, honor is a bigger category than obedience; it has to do with public acknowledgment of the parental role. Honor has to do with respect. How often do we allow our kids to be disrespectful? Sometimes it seems that teenagers today in the United States are expected and even encouraged to be disrespectful and rebellious. People often laugh, commenting that teenagers always act in such ways. They might, but should they?

Honoring parents in the ancient world also involved caring for elderly parents, and individualistic societies (like much of the United States) often do not prioritize this parental support. We often do not honor our parents and grandparents. Our dominant culture is structured in ways that make the giving of such honor difficult, including the notion that everyone should live independently (rather than in dependent—but not codependent—community). To what degree is independence a biblical value? Perhaps to an extent, but are we created to live life on our own, or are we created to be in community? My close female friends and I always say that before we married our husbands, we thought that we were pretty holy, unselfish people. Marriage really shines a spotlight on self-centeredness, as now I have to compromise instead of always getting my own way. Then, after my friends and I had kids, we realized to an even greater degree how selfish we were. Parenthood, done well, is really about death to self. Parents rarely get to do what they want or to live on their own terms; the terms are now defined by the needs of a child, a literal dependent. I once told my own mother that she is probably the least selfish person I have ever known. Her response? "It's called being a parent, Holly." Parenting sucks the selfishness right out of you, and that is really, really good for our discipleship. It forces us to live in ways that are other-centered rather than self-centered. Of course, many societies today are more collective rather than individual, and in those spaces people live more closely in community. Perhaps they have much to teach those of us in individualized cultures. Marriage and children are not the only way for people in individualistic societies to be discipled well, of course. Jesus and Paul were single, and their lives of singleness were anything but self-centered. They lived in the middle of robust, messy community, not on the sidelines.

Today many people do not believe that their parents deserve honor. For example, adult children may not respect their parents because of choices those parents made, especially parenting choices. It is true that the less integrity a

---

11. God declares that honoring one's parents will lead to long life in the earth, which probably is not an individual guarantee—if I honor my parents, I can guarantee myself a life into my nineties—but a communal reality. In other words, children honoring parents is a healthy family structure that is good for the larger health and longevity of communities and societies.

parent has, the more difficult it will be to honor them. However, it may be helpful to remember that honor in the ancient Mediterranean world was not as directly connected to feelings as it may be for us. Honor had to do with public acknowledgment of someone's status or role. You can still acknowledge your mother as your mother, even in public, whether or not she "deserves" it. You can still choose to speak about her respectfully, even if she does not return that respect. And you can celebrate your many, many brothers and sisters in Christ and the New Testament's expansion of what it means to be a family, centered on Jesus (Luke 8:19–21; 12:49–53; 18:29–30).

Much is required of children, but perhaps even more is required of parents. Paul commands parents, **Do not embitter your children, or they will become discouraged** (3:21). Paul literally addresses **fathers** (*patēr*) here, probably because, as I noted above, fathers (not mothers) had the primary cultural and legal authority over children in Paul's day. However, in the prior verse Paul does not use "father"; he uses the word "parents" (*goneus* [v. 20]), showing that mothers are involved and accountable in their parenting as well. Because fathers had more cultural power, Paul may actually be calling out first-century fathers here. In other words, he may be saying, "Okay, moms and dads, both of you are in this and need to parent well. However, dads, since you have more power in the Roman Empire, you need to be extra careful not to misuse it. Kids do need to be parented, but you need to consider your child's well-being in a bigger way. This may feel revolutionary, but following Jesus requires this of you. It's not just about the child, but it is also not just about you. It is about both of you, together, and how you treat each other."

Think about how often a person needs to be provoked or treated in ways that embitter them before they **become discouraged** (v. 21). Paul's point is that parents should not, *must not*, goad children into a state of ongoing resentment, make unreasonable demands (exhibited today through the ways that some parents attempt to live vicariously through their children athletically, musically, academically, etc.), overcorrect, harshly discipline, abuse authority, be unfair, humiliate children, or treat them disrespectfully. Do we ever model disrespect for our kids and then wonder why they are disrespectful to us? I have occasionally seen parents in public places (grocery stores, parks, etc.) who yell, and even swear, at their kids. Their kids return the yelling, and then the parents yell again, telling the children how disrespectful it is. I do not want that pattern to be my pattern.

I was not raised in a house where people yelled, so it surprised me when I started having kids and realized that yelling was one of my default responses to frustration. I remember one occasion when I was home with my one-year-old and three-year-old boys. They made a mess—I cannot remember if it was accidental or intentional—and I yelled. I yelled for a couple of minutes, telling them how they made poor decisions. I also told them how upset I was and how parenting was too hard for me. I was crying, and by the end my three-year-old was crying as well. His tears really impacted me, and I apologized immediately to both boys and pulled them in for a hug. That night I told my husband what had happened. I admitted that it scared me. I did not want to be someone who yells. I did not want my kids to grow up and remember me as a mom who yelled. Right then my husband committed to helping me stop that behavior, and that was the first time we agreed that, in our parenting generally, if either one of us saw the other parent forming a pattern of overcorrecting or otherwise inappropriately treating our children, we needed to say something (in private, not in front of the kids). We decided we needed to catch that behavior before it turned into a lifestyle, one that harmed not just us but our kids. We decided that we would both pray that God would help me to stop yelling but also that if I felt like yelling, I would take three deep breaths first. Those were the first steps to building a different pattern, a pattern where I can now—almost always—respond to my kids in calm ways. Thank you, Jesus.

My responses, of course, include discipline. Kids need to be disciplined; they need negative consequences when deserved, including in their own discipleship. But they need positive consequences as well. Parents, it is our job to teach our kids about God and what it means to follow Jesus and listen to the Spirit! We are their primary teachers, and our greatest responsibility is to form our children as disciples of Jesus. When my oldest son was little, he had a problem with interrupting. He would interrupt anyone, at any time, if he wanted to say something. My husband and I knew that we could not allow that to continue and become a pattern in his life, so we set a new expectation: if others were talking and he wanted to say something, he needed to raise his hand first. (That is the expectation in a classroom, after all.) It took some practice, but it worked. For a while he went through a phase where if we did not recognize that his hand was raised and respond quickly enough, he would use his other hand to slap his raised hand. The noise directed all attention to him, giving him the chance to speak. We applauded his creativity but insisted that he wait quietly. We also told him that we promised to be more attentive to him so that he would not have to wait so long.

In parenting, as in life and discipleship more generally, we need both grace and truth. If we lean too far toward grace in parenting, it can result in a free-for-all. Kids will raise themselves, do whatever they want, make all their own decisions, and so on. Sometimes I hear our culture saying that we should not impose our values on our kids, that kids should decide for themselves. This sounds like too much grace and like a forfeiting of our responsibilities as parents.

Should our kids be allowed to choose their own diets, their own levels of physical activity, their own amounts of screen time, how much they sleep, how they spend their time more generally, and whether they learn about God and commit to a local church? Many kids would definitely choose a diet without fruits and vegetables and with unlimited screen time.

I have heard that millennial parents often run their family lives democratically. Everyone gets an equal vote, including all the kids. That may work for an occasional Saturday activity like whether we hike or go to the beach, but will that vote determine how committed we are to our church, our Jesus-community? Will our kids' vote determine whether we participate and how deeply we do? How will this affect our explanations of *why* we do these things? That sounds risky to me. We often tell our kids (and remind ourselves) that we are our kids' *parents*, not our kids' *friends*. God gave us the job of parenting them. We need not only to raise them to be responsible adults; we also need to do our part to help them become fully devoted followers of Jesus who live in the power of the Spirit.

When we lean too far toward truth in parenting, though, what happens? It can become a "My way or the highway" or "No mistakes allowed" situation. Who wants to be part of that kind of family, where there is no grace, no real forgiveness? I have some friends who were raised in families where they felt like they could never live up to the standard that their parents set. Any mistake was a major setback, and they were reminded constantly of those mistakes. The parents did not apologize, nor did they offer reasons for why the kids were supposed to meet certain expectations. Such parenting can breed a culture of discouragement (Col. 3:21), among other things.

How can we live out the truth of Col. 3:20–21 today in ways that make sense in our cultural contexts? Households in the ancient Mediterranean were considered public spaces, not private, so the question for us is how we might model peace and respect in parent-child relationships in ways that publicly (not just privately!) testify to who Jesus is and what he has accomplished. It means that we discern what we can keep from our culture and what we must refuse. Part of Paul's point is that Christian parents are supposed to be different from non-Christian parents. Are we actually succeeding? Also, in Christian families both parents and children have responsibilities. It is good news that we are not alone in this. We have the church. The church also carries the responsibility to teach, nurture, and give responsibility to children, not simply ignore or tolerate them (but also not put them at the center, as if the world revolves around them). Our local churches must teach our kids what the Bible says and what God values. To be a Christian means to submit to God's vision and give up our own if it is in conflict with God's. We do this because this is the direction in which the Spirit leads us. In our parenting, to be led by the Spirit is to be attentive to the Spirit's direction both in Scripture and in any given moment. Often, in situations with my kids, I pray silently (and desperately!), "Spirit of God, give me the words to say here. Help me know what to do."

The last section of the household code speaks to slaves and masters (see the extended comments on slavery in the introduction). As Craig Keener notes, when we compare the three sections—wife/husband, child/parent, slave/master—we notice that "only the slave section is expanded beyond brief comment, which in turn allows fuller observation of Paul's intention."[12] It is also helpful to note that people in a household may have filled more than one role in the household code: for example, a slave might also be a child or a parent; a husband might be enslaved.[13] Colossians 3:22–4:1, the section on slaves and masters, reads as follows:

> **Slaves, obey your earthly masters in everything; and do it, not only when their eye is on you and to curry their favor, but with sincerity of heart and reverence for the Lord. Whatever you do, work at it with all your heart, as working for the Lord, not for human masters, since you know that you will receive an inheritance from the Lord as a reward. It is the Lord Christ you are serving. Anyone who does wrong will be repaid for their wrongs, and there is no favoritism. Masters, provide your slaves with what is right and fair, because you know that you also have a Master in heaven.**

Several years ago, my husband and I helped to plant a church. At a meeting for the leadership team I commented that many people in our church needed to change an aspect of how they lived out their faith. One of the other leaders said to me, "You're a leader. Take them there. Lead them there." I sat there, stunned, partly because I realized that it was true; that was part of my responsibility. But there was also something darker. I realized that I did not want to do it that way. It sounded hard, slow. It sounded like it would take work and energy that I did not have. It sounded complicated. Instead of leading by teaching and example, I wanted to say, "Stop doing what you're doing. It's stupid. Do this other thing instead." I wanted to do it the easy way.

The big question for us is this: In discipleship, how hard can we push one another so that we become more and more like Jesus? Within the context of relationship, how hard is too hard to push?

How would you feel if someone you barely know told you that something you believe is stupid? Oh, wait—that happens on social media all the time!

12. Keener, "Mutual Submission."
13. MacDonald, *Power of Children*, 33.

How do you receive that? Is your gut impulse to respond by saying, "Thanks! I am so happy to know that this idea I believe is stupid, and now I'll do it the way you want me to do it." I bet not. How would you feel if someone you know well—your sister, your spouse, your best friend—told you that something you believe is stupid? Does that change the dynamic? It might be a little better, but not much. In our marriage, my husband and I can push back pretty hard on each other, but we do not ever use "stupid" language. It is a nonstarter for us.

This matters because in Colossians (as in all his other letters) Paul is *discipling*. How hard does he push here in Col. 3:22–4:1, in the process of discipleship? This is a complicated text because the topic here is slaves and masters, and our world has recently experienced a global reckoning on racial issues, with the United States' history of slavery in the center of it. We are probably more communally aware of this history than we have ever been. Because of that reality it would be easy to ignore a text like this; it is complicated, is messy, and could be hurtful. However, avoiding texts that are challenging is not a solution either. Perhaps a better solution lies in the opposite direction. Maybe now is the time to do more than a surface read of Col. 3:22–4:1 and to think deeply and contextually about this text.

I am going to invert this passage and read the part about masters first, because his subversion of some important cultural standards and stereotypes is most obvious there. Colossians 4:1 reads, **Masters, provide your slaves with justice and equality, because you know that you also have a Master in heaven** (AT).

The fact that Paul tells masters that *they* have a master would have been shocking in the ancient world, as most masters did not have a master (though some slaves did own slaves). However, he is reminding them that if they are Jesus-people, they have an ultimate master. He also tells masters to provide their slaves with **justice and equality**. The Greek words here for "justice" (*dikaios*) and "equality" (*isotēs*)[14] are quite surprising, as this was language typically used for free people, not enslaved people. The philosopher Aristotle, for example, argued that slaves are inferior by nature, which means that injustice does not apply if someone is owned rather than free. Not everyone agreed with him, but Aristotle was an influential voice in the ancient Mediterranean world.

However, Paul's comment here makes sense in light of what he stated in 3:11, that there is no "slave or free," which makes such worldly distinctions insignificant for those who are part of the Creator's image-renewing project (see also Lev. 25:43, 53). Paul is basically saying, "Alright, masters, your master is watching you, and he cares about justice and equality. It would be wise to live in light of that, because that can be either good news or bad news for you.

14. See Vasser, "Grant Slaves Equality."

Justice sometimes involves judgment, after all." In this way Paul is on the most radical edge of ancient thinkers on the topic of slavery.

If we hear this as twenty-first-century people, we may think that Paul should do a better job because this is not radical enough. We may think that Paul should say what we would say today, which is that it is so obvious that slavery is a terrible and unjust system. That is a common and appropriate Christian viewpoint in our century, but how often did people say those kinds of things in the ancient Mediterranean world? Is it fair for us to expect them to share our view?

In his time and place, Paul is joining a few other Jewish voices that are, in their own ways, resisting slavery. These voices insisted that slaves should be treated better, that masters are held to standards as well. We have a few of these voices outside Jewish circles (including the Roman philosopher Seneca) but more in Jewish circles, and Paul is joining that movement of resistance. Such resistance might feel too small for us. We might wonder why Paul doesn't resist more strongly. Why didn't he gather a massive crew of people together to elect the right leaders who then could overhaul the system or even abolish it? Or why didn't he organize an antislavery protest, starting his own movement to abolish it? The short answer is that there were no public voices in that time that called for abolition of slavery as a system; slavery was the cultural default. Of course, in the Roman Empire the people did not elect their leaders or give input into how their political or cultural systems were set up. The emperor became emperor through specific uses of (usually military) power. So what does Paul do? He engages in what we might call small acts. He pursues local discipleship in local contexts. Sometimes this can be much more radical (see the comments on Philemon below, which also connect to slavery; see also 1 Cor. 7:21), but here in Colossae, in a church that Paul did not help to plant and does not know well, Paul pursues a more careful option. My suggestion is that we imagine our way into Paul's world and view this text from the perspective of the masters, who had legal power over their slaves. If this text is a *challenge to masters* and *not a weapon against slaves*, what would it cost masters to follow Paul's teaching here? What would it cost them to follow Jesus? If masters actually started treating slaves differently, with justice and equality (which could eventually lead to manumission, or freedom), how might other slave owners respond? What would be the social cost, and even the economic cost, if the social cost affected not just your reputation but your business?

Now, to slaves. In Col. 3:22–25 Paul says,

Slaves, obey your earthly masters in everything; and do it, not only when their eye is on you and to curry their favor, but with sincerity of heart and reverence for the Lord. Whatever you do, work at it with all your heart, as working for the

Lord, not for human masters, since you know that you will receive an inheritance from the Lord as a reward. It is the Lord Christ you are serving. Anyone who does wrong will be repaid for their wrongs, and there is no favoritism.

How do we make sense of this in a healthy way? First, as above with women and children, Paul here talks directly to those who are enslaved, not just about them. He treats them as responsible humans who can make their own choices and have agency. Typically, in household codes the master, often a male (though women could also own slaves), was addressed.

Paul does tell the enslaved people to **obey** (*hypakouō*), just as children are to "obey" (*hypakouō*) (v. 20), and to do so **in everything** (v. 22).[15] Paul also encourages a kind of obedience that applies even when the human master is not watching, because the heavenly master is watching. The word for "master" and "Lord" here is the same: *kyrios*. That "supervision" by Jesus stimulates a **sincerity of heart** (v. 22), an action that is done for the right reason. At least part of the right reason here is a frank reverence for or fear of the Lord. In the Bible the fear of the Lord is a common theme (for example, Ps. 111:10; Prov. 9:10). Those who do not fear the Lord do not act wisely. Fear is not blank terror but rather a proper understanding and even awe of God that realizes and respects who God is and who we are. God is God, and we are not. God is the master, and we are not. Remember, Paul reminds the human masters that God is their ultimate master. If slaves and masters both have the same ultimate master, what does that mean? Here Paul is playing with some of the lines that humans use to separate themselves and make distinctions about where people rank and how important they are: masters up top, slaves down low. But if Jesus is the master and other masters and slaves are all slaves, then that truth reshuffles people, as Paul says in Col. 3:11.

And yet, paradoxically, Jesus is not just the master but the slave. Jesus knows what slave treatment entails, as slaves were one of two main categories of people who were crucified. Slaves would be crucified if they ran away or were seen to deserve the ultimate punishment. The other category was that of rebel, those who rebelled against the power of Rome. In other words, Rome saw these people as terrorists and executed them accordingly. Jesus literally did a slave's death, and in some of Paul's other letters he stresses the point that Jesus has taken on slave qualities and realities (for example, Phil. 2:7). This is supposed to be

---

15. Margaret MacDonald stresses that a Christian slave might be forced to have sex with a master, which raises the question of God's judgment on sexual immorality (see Col. 3:5) ("Slavery, Sexuality"). My own view is that such acts of sexual assault would place the judgment on the master alone, not on the slave. The slave is not morally responsible for an act over which he or she has no choice. We might even say that the master has sinned against the slave; the slave has not sinned.

encouraging, of course; the true master knows the slave's situation deeply and personally.

Paul adds another comment that in some ways repeats what he just said to the slaves, though it also is reminiscent of what he said six verses earlier to the entire church at Colossae. To the entire church, he said, "And whatever you do, whether in word or deed, do it all in the name of the Lord Jesus, giving thanks to God the Father through him" (Col. 3:17). Now, to the slaves, he says, **Whatever you do, work at it with all your heart, as working for the Lord, not for human masters** (v. 23). In other words, what is true for all Christians is true for slaves as well. Even though slaves face more injustice and inequality when working for human masters than others do, Paul reminds them that they are actually working for their true Master, their true Lord. And that Master cares deeply about justice and equality (4:1). In other words, Paul here is adapting the basic format of the household code by putting Jesus at the center of it: Jesus is now *in, through, and above* the household, and that changes everything. Ancient Mediterranean people would have seen these changes and understood their significance.

In the Jesus-community, we do not maintain these kinds of distinctions *as a way to stratify people*. Paul is arguing something in a nuanced and complex way here; he is working in the tension between the ideal and the reality. The ideal—what's actually true in Jesus—is that Jews are not more important than gentiles (and vice versa) and masters are not more important than slaves (and vice versa) (3:11; see also Gal. 3:28). But then the reality is that Paul lives in a world where slavery is everywhere and people just assume that the world works that way. Even people who are followers of Jesus are living in that cultural context. So how do you move people *from* the reality of what is (how they are living because it is culturally normal) and *closer to* the vision of what is actually true in Jesus? Do you tell people that they are stupid or that they are obviously doing it the wrong way? Is that ever a persuasive way to communicate? If we want people to buy in, if we want to persuade people to join the Jesus-vision, perhaps we need to do it differently. Maybe instead of attempting to make people cross the entire distance from where they are to where they should be in one leap, we should move people a step or two closer to the vision. The next time you talk to them, you can move them a step or two closer again. I think this is what Paul is doing here in Col. 3. And we call this discipleship.

There are a few other surprising aspects to this passage that we should also note. First, Paul reminds the slaves that they *know* they have **an inheritance** [*klēronomia*] **from the Lord as a reward** (3:24; see also 1:12 for "inheritance" language). The New Testament uses "inheritance" language often to talk about the kingdom of God.[16] "Kingdom of God" is a Jewish way of saying, "Everyone, God sees all the brokenness in the world, all the way from Holly's personal brokenness up to systemic brokenness. God sees it all, and God is working to fix it. The New Testament insists that Jesus is at the center of that fixing. God's doing it in and through Jesus. And someday that's going to be finished. God's restorative project is going to be complete (in new creation)."[17] Paul is reminding the Christian slaves here that they have this inheritance waiting for them; this is a long-game, big-picture perspective that he is asking them to maintain, even if their present reality is difficult. This is a powerful image because slaves did not inherit in the Roman Empire; children inherited, heirs inherited. Paul is reminding these slaves that though they may be property in the eyes of some, in reality they are sons and daughters. God's project of restoration, his new creation, will be theirs fully someday, even if now it is partial.[18]

Paul loves to make the point that everyone is a slave to something or someone, and he does so again here: **It is the Lord Christ you are serving** (3:24). The word for "serving" is *douleuō*, which is the verb that is related to the noun *doulos* ("slave"). In the next chapter *doulos* is used of Epaphras as a "slave" of Christ (4:12) (the related word *syndoulos* is used of both Epaphras and Tychicus to describe each being a "fellow slave" in the Lord [1:7; 4:7]). Slaves serve their masters; it is their job. Here Paul stresses again that their true master is Jesus, not a human master. This is powerful because it shows how in the household code Paul's ultimate focus is *not* on the male husband, parent, and master in the household but rather on the lordship of Christ as Master. "Paul's discussion of household relationships therefore is an application of his general call to recognize Jesus as the Lord of all."[19] Said differently, "If we confess Jesus Christ as our 'Lord,' we are acknowledging that we are his 'slaves.'"[20]

Paul also warns slaves not to do wrong: **Anyone who does wrong will be repaid for their wrongs, and there is no favoritism** (3:25). He basically is telling them, "Judgment comes. Your true master is watching." Many people today do not like the idea of Paul telling slaves not to do wrong when others have wronged them so deeply. There is a great deal that I could say on the topic, but at least one important question to ask is whether anyone wronged Jesus. How did he respond? Did he do wrong back? The desire to pay back, and perhaps even to escalate the situation, is most often our human default because the person or

16. See, for example, Acts 20:32; Gal. 3:18; Eph. 1:14; 5:5; Heb. 9:15; 1 Pet. 1:4.

17. See also the sidebar "Defining the Gospel" at Col. 1:5.

18. Sylvia Keesmaat points out that in Jewish tradition enslaved people were able to inherit at the Jubilee Year, when they were released and became free (Lev. 25) ("Colossians," 568). This shapes the way that Jews, including Jesus, understood the inheritance of the kingdom of God.

19. Pao, "Serving Our Master," 103.

20. Pao, "Serving Our Master," 103.

group "deserves" it. But here Paul reminds us that "getting back" is not how the kingdom of God works. Followers of Jesus are to live as Jesus lived (1 John 2:6). This is a hard word for a world filled with injustice but also with vengeance. Christians are called to live another way, walking behind Jesus in the way of discipleship, taking another step, then another—walking closer to our future.

Paul concludes his instructions to slaves here by reminding them that **there is no favoritism** (Col. 3:25; see also Acts 10:34). God does not have favorites, which means that God judges impartially, treating everyone, including slaves and masters, in the same way (see also 2 Cor. 5:10). Of course, in Paul's day slaves lived in a worldly reality that was very different; clearly, they were not anyone's favorite. They ranked at the bottom. Masters, not slaves, were favorites. Paul insists, however, that this is not their or our future. In the kingdom of God the inheritance levels out all these unlevel realities. The very next verse details Paul's instructions to masters (4:1), which I have already discussed. There Paul commands masters to provide justice and equality for their slaves. Paul is basically saying, "Jesus is watching, so live well. Remember, human masters, not to do wrong, because judgment comes. There is no favoritism. Take another step in the right direction."

The big-picture question remains for us: In discipleship, how do we push well, correct well, guide well? How hard can we push? How do we move people *from* the realities of where they are, ourselves from where we are, and closer *to* what is true in Jesus and where God is taking the world? If we are asking these questions, we are seeing the household code as a challenge to us and not as a weapon. The household codes have often been weaponized and used to legitimate abuses of other people, especially women and slaves. They have even been used in the United States to justify the institution of slavery itself, as if God were proslavery! That history needs to be acknowledged because of the deep harm that has been done. It is not okay. But that is not all there is to say.

Honestly, I wish that Paul would have gone further. I wish that he had been more radical in Colossians than he is. This text is easier to weaponize than some other New Testament texts. But if I stop there, if I do not ask some of the other questions that are important, then I have not given Paul, and this text in Colossians, a fair shot. What does it mean for us to honor the reality that we are not the first recipients of this letter? That it was not written to us first? It is part of Scripture and is ours, but it was not ours first. Are we just going to take it and say, "We don't care who the original recipients were. It's ours now, and we're going to read it how we wish"? If we do that, we can miss that what Paul actually said expressed one of the most radically antislavery sentiments of his day. He was not talking about overthrowing the institution of slavery, whether with legislation (as that was not an option for them) or violence (as that does not fit with New Testament teaching in general); even the failed slave revolts of his era had never attempted to eliminate the institution. The Romans were famous for efficiently and bloodily quenching any hint of rebellion. But Paul most certainly was charting a new path of resistance to slavery for followers of Jesus. The ancient Greco-Roman context would have understood this reality, especially since discussions of the household typically included commands to worship various gods or goddesses. The defiance that Colossians brings lies in its proclamation of another God and his kingdom: the command to "do it all in the name of the Lord Jesus" (3:17) includes how we live in the household.

The Letters to the Colossians and to Philemon are related because Philemon was a member of the church in Colossae. If the Letter to Philemon was written first, and Philemon responded by freeing Onesimus, then the Letter to the Colossians was delivered to them *by a freed slave* (Col. 4:9 [see comments there]). If both letters were delivered at the same time, then Onesimus would have stood before them as the one whom Paul asked Philemon to treat as a brother, not as a slave. If Colossians was written first, then Paul was paving the way for an even more radical subversion of slavery in Philemon. No matter the order of the letters, the call to masters in Col. 4:1 to enact justice and equality for slaves would have been connected to the slave Onesimus himself. What a powerful challenge and testimony!

The household code in Colossians offers us at least three discipleship points as we navigate the path of discipleship together and navigate the tension between what is ideal because it is true in Jesus and what our current realities are. The first is more specific to the text, whereas the second two are more general. In our contexts today, we have a higher call in living toward God's kingdom because we can enact it in ways that ancient Mediterranean people could not. We can and should resist injustice and inequality in all kinds of public ways, as the world is watching us. For example, many of us in the so-called West benefit from our own versions of slavery in other parts of the world. For example, slave-like working conditions allow us to buy cheap shoes, electronic devices, and coffee. We must find creative ways, both individually and communally, to resist such injustice.

Second, and more generally, is God calling us to push back on or challenge other Christians, especially in terms of equality and justice? In other words, how might God want to use us to help disciple another Christian or group? How can we do that well so that what we say will be heard well? Paul does *not* walk into these situations and say, "You're stupid. Stop it." He *does* persuade. He does push buttons. He does challenge and subvert. But he wants an audience who will listen to him. And third, how will we respond if someone challenges us in our discipleship, especially regarding justice and equality? How can we give people the benefit of the doubt, especially our brothers and sisters in Christ, those who want to help us get closer to the future inheritance that God has for all of us? In other words, how can we be realistic about where people are—where we are—in the discipleship journey but also be part of the process of bringing them closer to where God wants them and us to be? Said differently, How do we participate well in this image-renewing restorative project God is enacting for the world (3:10)? So we say to the Father, Son, and Holy Spirit, "We know that you are speaking. We know that you do not stop speaking. We ask that you speak to us through this complicated text. Speak. Move. And give us soft hearts so that we are receptive to what you are saying and live differently because of it, even in and through the household code."

Embodying the Reality (3)

Embodying Christ in the World

In the final instructions Paul (and Timothy) moves from how to live in Christian community and the home (3:1–4:1) to how to live in the world (4:2–6). Here two themes from earlier in the letter appear again: prayer and thankfulness. In the beginning of the letter Paul and Timothy declare, "We *always thank* God, the Father of our Lord Jesus Christ, when we *pray* for you" (1:3). Several verses later a similar point is made again: "For this reason, since the day we heard about you, we have *not stopped praying* for you" (v. 9). In the third chapter the focus is thankfulness: "Let the peace of Christ rule in your hearts, since as members of one body you were called to peace. And *be thankful*" (3:15).[1]

What we see in this passage, once again, is a pattern of Paul and his coworkers living in certain ways—here, in ongoing prayer and thankfulness—with the expectation that other followers of Jesus should also live in these ways. In other words, Paul and the people around him are not special The practices they are engaged in are not possible or healthy only for leaders or "extra holy" ones; rather, they are leading by example, and others should follow. They model what they teach. Do we? This is a relevant question to ask in all areas of teaching (including money, sacrifice, service, etc.), but the topics at hand are quite powerful. I have learned in my own life that I can pray briefly, in snippets, throughout the day as I feed my family, do job-related work, do laundry, and so forth. However, I experience a much deeper sense of communion with God if

---

1. Paul also encourages thankfulness in Col. 1:12 and in other letters as well; see, for example, Rom. 7:25; 1 Cor. 14:18; Phil. 1:3; Philem. 4.

I have a more extended time to pray, and for years I struggled to find that time. I know that for many people early mornings are best. I am still not a morning person (ask my husband!), even after having kids and working a day job. I am simply not at my best in the early mornings. Then, one day, I sensed the Spirit pointing out to me that my commute gives me time. On my drive to and from work I would typically listen to music or think about what I had to do that day, but the Spirit pointed out that I could pray during that time. Now I sometimes even look forward to my commute because it gives me time to pray. There is a deep irony here for me, as I am someone who has profoundly disliked my commute in the past and does not like to drive; in my ideal world, I would walk to work. I have been so surprised that God has redeemed that experience for me by helping me to see how I could use the time well. Of course, that is how God works. God can redeem anything.

Here, near the end of the Letter to the Colossians, Paul (and Timothy) returns to his earlier themes, commanding followers of Jesus: **Devote yourselves to prayer, being watchful and thankful** (4:2; see comments on prayer at 1:3, 9; see also Jesus's instructions in Mark 14:38; Luke 18:1). We know what devotion looks like; it is consistency, perseverance, long-term pursuit. I find this deeply encouraging, actually, because I can pursue prayer long-term even if I miss a day sometimes, or pray shallowly sometimes, or do not enjoy every moment of it. I can persevere through the highs and lows and still be faithful.

I can also be **watchful and thankful**, following the example of Timothy and Paul, who arguably had a much harder life than I have had. We watch or pay attention, noting how God answers prayers as we also await the second coming of Christ. We also practice thankfulness or gratitude, as noted above (1:3; 3:15 [see comments there]). Thankfulness is a very different posture than fear, for example. Many ancient Mediterranean people prayed to various gods and goddesses out of fear, attempting to encourage or manipulate a deity into acting. Living in gratitude, in contrast, sharpens our awareness of current blessings in our lives and focuses our prayers in healthy ways, making us less likely to pray selfishly and more likely to pray for others and the world, and for ourselves, in God-honoring rather than self-centered ways (that focus on wants rather than needs, for example).

The focus on prayer continues, as the Colossians are asked to pray for Paul and Timothy (4:3). I love the idea of Paul asking for prayer. Honestly, I love the idea that even Paul needs prayer. Sometimes Paul seems like some kind of superhero, as if he were immune to the pressures and struggles and lack of clarity that the rest of us face in daily life. But no, Paul needs prayer, and he is vulnerable enough to ask for it. The prayer is specific, and his request is *not* that his persecution and imprisonment would end. Instead, he says, **And pray for**

us, too, that God may open a door for our message, so that we may proclaim the mystery of Christ, for which I am in chains. Pray that I may proclaim it clearly, as I should (4:3–4). Even though Paul is in prison (see also Eph. 3:1; 4:1; Phil. 1:12–14; Philem. 1, 9, 23), which is difficult, he is actually asking for prayer not for himself but for others, because his deepest desire and goal is for other people to join him in the Jesus-movement. He and Timothy need an open door (see also Acts 14:27; 1 Cor. 16:9; 2 Cor. 2:12), good opportunities, to share the truth of the **mystery of Christ**. We have already seen this language in Colossians (1:26–27; 2:2), and "mystery" is used again here in chapter 4 to describe a reality that used to be secret (only God knew) but has been revealed to humans now in and through what Jesus has done. In other words, the mystery is no longer a mystery.

The mystery in Paul's letters is associated with God's inclusion of gentiles in salvation in and through Jesus and is both present- and future-oriented. Christ will accomplish our promised future, a future that has already begun in the present as we—Jews and non-Jews—die with Christ and are raised to new life, a life of image-renewing discipleship that will find its conclusion when the restoration of creation (including nonhuman creation) is complete and we live in perfect union with our Creator (see also comments at 1:26–27;

Persecution Today

When Christians are persecuted today, distinctions are not often made between charismatic/pentecostal and noncharismatic/nonpentecostal believers. While Christians in the United States, Canada, and western Europe may face various kinds of verbal persecution, less often is the persecution physical. The church in the majority world, however, does face physical persecution at times. The January 2021 edition of the *Church of God Evangel* tells the following story: "On October 1, 2020, in India's Chattisgarh state, 10 Christian families were summoned to a village meeting in Gadada, where they were told to recant their faith or face dire consequences. Before they could answer, a mob attacked these Christians. Bone fractures, head injuries, and hearing loss were among the injuries, according to Pastor Susheel Kumar."[a] This is but one story among many, of course.

a. Colkmire, "Bow or Burn," 13.

2:2). Paul is deeply committed to this mystery, and it is the reason why he is in prison. Are we as deeply committed to the mystery of Christ, to the hope that Jesus brings? I know that there are many Christians in the past and in our current world who have sacrificed so much more than I have to participate in God's restorative mystery. I am both inspired and humbled by these brothers and sisters in Christ. Quite honestly, I need to pray for them more often. I do not do it often enough.

Paul's concluding prayer request is incredibly compelling: **Pray that I may proclaim it** [the mystery] **clearly, as I should** (4:4). Even Paul needs the Spirit's empowerment to speak, preach, and teach well! Clarity in communication is necessary. Here the word "should" represents the Greek word *dei*, which has the sense of being *necessary* or that it *must* be the case (also in v. 6). In other words, Paul feels a deep compulsion to proclaim the truth well, but even he is at risk of being unclear, of bumbling the message, of putting up unnecessary obstacles in his invitation to others to join the Jesus-movement. This reality is encouraging to me, as I am aware that I cannot speak and teach in my own power very well. I often pray—before walking into my classroom, before having lunch with a student or friend, even during a conversation that suddenly provides an opening for me to talk about Jesus—that the Spirit will help me to communicate well, be articulate in ways that make sense *in that setting*, and speak the words that people need to hear. The setting matters a great deal because, of course, speaking to college students (at least some of whom are not followers of Jesus) in an academic setting is different from speaking to my kids (as they are still trying to understand what their own commitments to Jesus mean, including what that means for how they live), which is different from talking with my non-Christian neighbors (who generally are not impressed with Christians but do appreciate our family). I try not to assume that I will **proclaim it clearly, as I should** (4:4); I pray that the Spirit will help me to do it. Sometimes I ask others to pray for me as well. I have learned that whenever I start feeling too confident in my own abilities, I am pretty much guaranteed to be unclear and unhelpful in an important conversation or teaching moment. Those experiences always humble me and send me again in pursuit of the Spirit's empowerment rather than my own.

Just as Paul and Timothy ask for prayer to be appropriately missional and invitational toward outsiders, now Paul commands us to do the same: **Be wise in the way you act toward outsiders; make the most of every opportunity. Let your conversation be always full of grace, seasoned with salt, so that you may know how to answer everyone** (4:5–6). We are to be wise in the way we act toward those who do not (yet) follow Jesus, and we are to live this way consistently. As earlier in the letter (2:6), the verb often translated as "walk" or "act" here is *peripateō*. Paul employs this word often when he is discussing our lifestyles, not onetime actions.[2] In the Letter to the Colossians we are told that wisdom is found in Christ (2:3) and is a gift from the Spirit (1:9, 28), making our reliance on the Spirit even more necessary.[3] This is a powerful challenge to those of us in pentecostal or charismatic contexts that often associate the Spirit's power with gifts such as tongues or compelling preaching but not with the quiet, seemingly unremarkable conversations that we might have with non-Christians at our jobs, in our neighborhoods, or at school. Spirit-imbued wisdom is also the power source behind nonverbal expressions of Christian witness, including practical support and meeting human needs such as hunger and medical care. Such actions can be a powerful witness to a God who deeply cares about the world and his image-renewing project.

What might it mean to **make the most of every opportunity** (4:5; see also Eph. 5:15–16)? The Greek verb here (*exagorazō*) is one that is often used to talk about purchasing worthwhile products in an eager and appropriate way; the energy behind such purchasing is part of the point. Think about the last time you really wanted to buy something that you thought was valuable. Your eagerness, your focus, your desire—all this guided you in your purchase of that cup of coffee, clothing, athletic equipment, book, or car. If your purchase was something lost (due to debt, perhaps) and then regained, the impact of the purchase is even greater; you have bought it back, ransomed it. That home is yours once again. The point here is that we should value opportunities with outsiders and approach them with eagerness, ready to pay the price (of time, of energy, of careful thought and prayer) that they demand. These encounters are critical, for the time is precious (the noun *kairos*, translated as **opportunity** in the NIV, is often employed to highlight special moments or seasons), and we should take advantage of them in the best possible way.

The best possible way means that our words must be **full of grace** (4:6; see also Eph. 4:29). In my current context, when I speak with non-Christians, I *begin* with the beauty of God's restorative and grace-filled work in the world, not with condemnation. God's grace in working to redeem takes center stage (compare Luke 4:22). If words are full of grace, they can be described as gracious. A gracious person is one who responds well even when slighted or treated poorly. They speak with respect even when someone speaks disrespectfully to them (see also Ps. 45:2; Eccles. 10:12). We all know how attractive this kind of person is. We want to be around them because their approach invites a positive response from us. We want not just to be *around* them but to be *like* them.

2. See, for example, Rom. 6:4; 13:13; 2 Cor. 4:2; 5:7; 12:18; Gal. 5:16; Eph. 2:2, 10; 4:1, 17; 5:2, 8, 15; Phil. 3:17–18; Col. 1:10; 3:7; 4:5; 1 Thess. 2:12; 4:1, 12; 2 Thess. 3:6, 11.

3. See also Luke 21:15; Acts 6:3, 10; 1 Cor. 12:8; Eph. 1:8; James 1:5; 3:13, 17; 2 Pet. 3:15.

Our words must also be **seasoned with salt** (4:6). The metaphor was common in the ancient world, and Jesus himself uses it (Matt. 5:13; Mark 9:49–50; Luke 14:34–35). It conveys a sense of tastiness. Salt preserves, of course, but it is also a seasoning that makes food delicious. When was the last time I talked to a non-Christian and spoke truth in a way that encouraged the other person to gobble up what I said? (Of course, too much salt has the opposite effect; no one wants to eat oversalted food.) In other words, the ideas of being "gracious" and "tasty" are similar; they encourage a positive response from the other person. Here Paul is deeply invested in us being good witnesses to Jesus in this way.

The point is for all of us to **know how to answer everyone** (4:6; see also 1 Pet. 3:15). Paul again here uses *dei*, the word that carries a sense of necessity (also in 4:4). I must know how to answer each person, and that will vary according to the person, of course. It is also true that if we are devoted to prayer (4:2), we will be better equipped to **know how to answer everyone** (v. 6). With my non-Christian neighbors, knowing how to answer them means at least partly that I must communicate in ways that show I care about some of the issues that matter to them—such as water usage in a drought-ridden California—and be able to demonstrate how my Christian faith is the reason why. The Creator God gave humans the task of managing creation (Gen. 1:26–27), which includes the water.[4] My family must practice that stewardship so that our neighbors can see it, which means that we must be consistent and embody what we say we believe.

When I talk with non-Christian students, I also must demonstrate that I care about and am aware of at least some of the issues that matter to them. For some students, there is one primary question; it may be about injustice generally, or a family member's illness or death, or a current cultural idea. Those students want to know what Christian faith has to say about their question. For other students, it is more about the Christian worldview. In other words, some have never heard (or seen) a positive presentation of the good news, God's image- and creation-renewing project. All that these students have been offered is a negative, scary, turn-or-burn kind of message, and they do not find it compelling. I do not know ahead of time what students need, of course. It is my task as a Christian to engage in a long enough and meaningful enough conversation that I, with the discernment that only the Spirit can provide, discover the need. Then, while praying silently, I attempt to offer words that are attractive and tasty. I want my words to be gobbled up. This does not mean, of course, that I never share a hard word or talk about judgment; that would be oversalting the food. Judgment is actually the other side of the justice coin and sometimes can be very encouraging in that it is God's answer to evil. It does mean that I am

---

4. See Richter, *Stewards of Eden*.

going to work hard not to set up *unnecessary* stumbling blocks. I *must* discern carefully how to answer each person, and being *unnecessarily* weird or harsh is not helpful and is opposed to the New Testament's teaching. This also means that we in the church cannot be a "holy huddle" but must be in regular relationship with outsiders, as such relationships offer opportunities to bear (both spoken and embodied) Christian witness. In relationship—a sharing of lives and stories—this testimony will not feel artificial or forced but instead like part of the natural rhythm.[5]

5. Dunn, *Epistles*, 266–68.

Final Greetings and Blessing

Paul next transitions to personal news and greetings (Col. 4:7–18), a section typical of ancient Mediterranean letters. In Colossians this portion is quite lengthy; it is twelve verses, and the entire letter contains only ninety-five verses. This is likely due at least partly to the fact that Paul did not help to plant the church in Colossae and does not know many of its members very well. In a culture that prioritizes community and relationships (this is true also of many contexts today in Africa, Asia, and Central and South America) rather than individual accomplishments and independence (as do many contexts in the United States, Canada, and Europe), it also makes sense for Paul to stress here, at the end of the letter, all the ways in which he (and Timothy!) and the Colossian Christians are relationally connected. Their communities overlap in powerful ways.

Paul first mentions Tychicus in 4:7: **Tychicus will tell you all the news about me. He is a dear brother, a faithful minister and fellow servant in the Lord** (Tychicus also appears in Acts 20:4; Eph. 6:21; 2 Tim. 4:12; Titus 3:12). Tychicus is clearly part of the Jesus-family, as Paul calls him a **dear brother** (*agapētos adelphos*). He is also a **faithful minister** (*pistos diakonos*) and **fellow servant** (*syndoulos*). In chapter 1 Epaphras, one of Paul's coworkers who helped to plant the church in Colossae, is described with this same language (1:7 [see comments there]; see also 4:12). Again, *diakonos* is the basis of the modern word "deacon" (though that office was a later development) and can be translated as "minister, servant, assistant, intermediary" (in 1:23, 25 Paul calls himself a *diakonos*). The use of "slave" language (*syndoulos*) also links Paul and Timothy to these lesser-known figures; they are fellow slaves. As I mentioned previously, though often translated as "fellow servant," *syndoulos* can be translated as "fellow slave," and in an ancient Mediterranean context where slavery was a constant reality, the point would be powerful, as slaves were owned by others. Paul uses "slave" language elsewhere to describe his own labor for God,[1] and he argues that everyone is a slave to something (for example, Rom. 6:16, 19), as he does in this letter as well (note "ruled by the flesh" in Col. 2:11).

Every time I read a text like this, I think, "I want to be a friend and coworker of Paul! How amazing it would be to be described in this way!" Paul uses this kind of language for both men and women, of course (see comments at 4:15). Imagine such a letter from Paul, with you named as a friend and coworker:

> Dear friends, Holly [*use your name in place of mine*] will update you on what is happening with me. She is a beloved sister in Christ who is faithfully ministering to all around her. Like me and all of you, she is Christ's slave. As a slave, she serves well, consistently honoring others above herself and inviting more people into Christ's image-renewing project. The Spirit guides her. She is wholly, truly dependent on the Spirit's presence and empowerment.

How does that make you feel? Does it scare you? Inspire you? Move you to tears? All of the above? What might it cost us to be Christ's slaves? Is that really who we want to be? Our selfish side may say no, but our image-being-renewed side says yes. Yes! How amazing it would be to be counted among Paul's friends in this way, to have contributed so meaningfully to putting off sin and putting on our true selves, which have been and are being reconciled to Christ. Perhaps we should identify most closely with people like this in the New Testament: small characters, seemingly random people about whom we know almost nothing. *We* know almost nothing, but their friends know, their communities know, and God knows.

One of the few things we know about Tychicus is that he is delivering the Letter to the Colossians (as he also does the Letter to the Ephesians [see Eph. 6:21–22]). That is why Paul can say that Tychicus will tell them all the news about Paul (Col. 4:7). Paul adds more detail in the following verse: **I am sending him to you for the express purpose that you may know about our circumstances and that he may encourage your hearts** (v. 8).[2] We wish we knew more about Paul's circumstances in prison, of course. What we do know is pieced together

---

1. See Rom. 1:1; 2 Cor. 4:5; Gal. 1:10; Phil. 1:1; Titus 1:1.

2. Some other ancient copies of Colossians have "that he may know" how you are (KJV, NIV text note) rather than "that you may know" how we are (NIV). Most scholars think that the second option is best because it fits with what Paul says in the verse prior about Tychicus bringing the news about Paul (v. 7).

The "Randos" and the "No-Names"

In the New Testament Paul is often seen as a "major" character, and understandably so. I wonder about the priorities that support such a focus, however. In other words, might some cultures that are shaped by an adoration of the hero figure—especially if that hero is surprising in any way—*focus* too much on seemingly heroic characters? In the United States we see such a focus in politics, in health care, in environmental issues, in sports, and in entertainment, among other areas. Christians often have their own version of the hero obsession, as exhibited in the focus on various pastors and other leaders. My question is this: Who is allowed to decide who the heroes are?

I have noticed that most Christians today tend to compare themselves to "major" characters in the Bible (for example, Moses, David, Peter, Paul)[a] and that this often creates stress and pressure to accomplish the "big" things that people like Paul accomplished. When we realize, however, that most of us are not going to save the world and be the hero, some of us stop contributing. We live however we wish, because we think that our faithful witness as just one person does not matter very much.

When I read the New Testament, I notice not just Paul but many, many people whom I call the "randos" and the "no-names." Again and again, I notice how their faithfulness contributes to the spread of the gospel. Their lives count. They are filled with the Holy Spirit, just like the major characters. Shouldn't charismatics and pentecostals also notice such figures, especially since we prioritize the ways in which the Spirit surprises us? Don't we insist that the Spirit empowers all, even those—perhaps especially those—who lack access to typical structures of power and influence?

Maybe a few of us will accomplish really impressive public feats, at least by some standards. Most of us, however, will live fairly ordinary lives, at least for our time and the cultures in which we live. We will work typical jobs, raise and/or participate in families, and be part of a local church. In other words, we will not be the hero. But maybe that's okay, because Jesus is the hero. Perhaps most of us are called to be faithful where we are—in small ways, in local contexts. Think about the new followers of Jesus in cities like Colossae. Someone shares the good news with them, or they see a local Jesus-community in action, and they join. They are in. But they don't change the world, at least not on their own. Maybe they change their neighborhood. Maybe they change their town. They keep raising kids, working as masons or fish sellers or bakers or day laborers, working dawn to dusk trying to get something to eat that day. Are their lives meaningful? Do they contribute to the growth and spread of the gospel by living their lives and participating in their local Jesus-community? Of course! Again and again in the New Testament people's small contributions—their local faithfulness—witness to their neighbors about who Jesus is·and what he cares about and what he is doing in the world through the power of the Holy Spirit.

Part of this is individual, and individual witness is important. I can testify to who God is and what God has done and is doing. I can model values with my life. But communal witness is near to God's heart because we are not created to be self-sustaining, self-identifying witnesses. We're created to live faith and embody commitment to Jesus together, in community in a local church. I literally cannot do it on my own. And neither can you.

a. In personal correspondence with Craig Keener, the coeditor of this commentary series, on September 13, 2023, he added, "We also tend to inflate them. Paul started home Bible studies in various towns, kept getting run out of town in many places, pastored some immature and contentious churches of new converts, etc. But apart from Jesus, virtually nobody in the Bible volunteered for their testing. Ultimately God was the only hero. Those with 'big' ministries went through 'big' tests beforehand (and sometimes during, like Paul's thorn in the flesh) so they would remember that it was God working in them, not their own worthiness."

from letters where Paul mentions his chains (see the introduction for discussion of Paul's imprisonments) and from the narrative of Paul's custody in books like Acts (Acts 22:23–28:31), which many connect to Paul's Prison Letters. Part of Tychicus's task is to encourage the hearts of the Colossian Christians, just as Paul expressed earlier in the letter (Col. 2:2). The "heart" in the Bible is the center of our will, our emotion, our very being. It is the core of who we are, and Paul's desire is that Tychicus will encourage the Colossians at their core. I am encouraged just thinking about this. I also wonder whether Tychicus did a good job. Did he encourage well? He would also have answered any questions that the Colossians asked about the letter, as this was part of the role of letter carriers (compare Phoebe in Rom. 16:1–2). In other words, only trusted people were given such a task. I love to imagine being part of that conversation. How encouraged would I be?

Tychicus is traveling to Colossae with the letter, but even he is not alone. Paul states in the next verse that someone else will be present: **Onesimus, our faithful and dear brother, who is one of you. They will tell you everything that is happening here** (4:9). Such news would include information about the church in Rome or wherever Paul is imprisoned.

Notice that Onesimus is not called a slave here; he is **our faithful and dear brother** (v. 9), which alludes to Philem. 16 and reminds us of Onesimus's true identity as part of the Jesus-family. It is likely that this Onesimus is the same one mentioned in the Letter to Philemon (Philem. 10) because he is described as a local (**one of you** [Col. 4:9]), just as Epaphras is a local (4:12). Epaphras is the one who introduced the Colossians to the good news about Jesus and what he accomplished, including inaugurating the kingdom of God (1:7). It makes sense that a local person would be well suited to evangelize their hometown because they understand the context intimately. The Letters to the Colossians and to Philemon share several names, which points toward the same community. Beyond Epaphras, there is Aristarchus (Col. 4:10; Philem. 24), Mark (Col. 4:10; Philem. 24), Luke (Col. 4:14; Philem. 24), Demas (Col. 4:14; Philem. 24), and Archippus (Col. 4:17; Philem. 2).

It is also likely that the Onesimus here is the same one as in Philemon because Paul describes him as a **dear brother** (*agapētos adelphos*); Paul uses the same language for Onesimus in Philem. 16 (*adelphos agapētos*). Paul also calls Onesimus "my very heart" (*ta ema splanchna*) in Philem. 12, a term of deep endearment (*splanchna* is used also at Col. 3:12 [see comments there]). We cannot be certain that the Onesimus in both letters is the same man, mainly because "Onesimus" was a common name (especially of slaves), but it is quite likely.

As already mentioned, Aristarchus appears next. Paul calls him **my fellow prisoner** and notes that Aristarchus sends greetings to the Colossians (4:10). Aristarchus appears not just in Colossians and Philem. 24 but also in Acts 19:29; 20:4; 27:2 (along with Timothy and Tychicus, among others) as part of the group that brings the financial collection from the gentile churches to the Jewish church in Judea, which is in danger of starving to death. Luke, the author of Acts, identifies Aristarchus's hometown as Thessalonica, in the province of Macedonia. In other words, he appears to have been present with and traveled with Paul for long periods, even sharing imprisonment with him. His labor as a coworker of Paul may have led to his imprisonment, or Aristarchus may have been sharing chains voluntarily, in solidarity with Paul. Both of these options are deeply compelling and raise questions for us. What kind of labor would we continue to do if imprisonment were the possible end? Many Christians in our world today are faced with this question on a regular basis. Perhaps even more pointedly, is there anyone with whom we would voluntarily share imprisonment, especially if that person were not blood family but Jesus-family?

Mark is also sending his greetings to the Colossians (Col. 4:10). Mark as he appears in the book of Acts is a favorite of mine (Acts 12:12, 25; 15:37, 39; see also 2 Tim. 4:11). This is because Mark seems to have grown up privileged (Mary, his mother, apparently ran her own household [Acts 12:12]) but ends up sacrificing his privilege and using it in the service of the kingdom of God, God's image-renewing project. In other words, he likely could have lived a fairly easy and mundane life, at least according to ancient standards, but his encounter with the hope found through Jesus changed everything. He traveled with Paul and Barnabas on their first "missionary journey" (Acts 12:25–15:39) but ended up parting ways with Paul "because he had deserted them in Pamphylia and had not continued with them in the work" (15:38). Barnabas, however, gave Mark another chance (v. 39). This makes even more sense if Mark and Barnabas were cousins (Col. 4:10; see also Acts 4:36). In other words, Mark is a favorite of mine because he was deeply compelled by the gospel and sacrificed a great deal to participate as a coworker in it, but he definitely made some mistakes, even deserting Paul and Barnabas! Later he seems to have reconciled with Paul, as Colossians and Philemon indicate (see also 2 Tim. 4:11); he is back with Paul, "slaving" and laboring for the gospel. Neither are our mistakes the end for us. Our mistakes, our moments where we forfeit the beauty of the gospel through our own poor choices and actions, do not need to define us. They did not define Mark, after all. According to church tradition, it is this Mark who wrote the Gospel of Mark in the New Testament. Later in his life he became a coworker of Peter, who calls him "my son" (1 Pet. 5:13), and he wrote down Peter's stories about Jesus in the Gospel of Mark. Wow! Even a screwup like Mark ended up being able to contribute to Jesus's work. There is hope for all of us.

Mark sends greetings and apparently hopes to visit the Colossians (they **have received instructions about him** and are to **welcome him** if he comes [4:10]). A man named **Jesus, who is called Justus, also sends greetings** (v. 11). Because he shares the name "Jesus," he likely has taken a nickname in order to differentiate himself. The name "Jesus" is the Greek version of the Hebrew name "Joshua," which means "God rescues." It was a popular name for Jewish boys in this time, as many Jewish parents were hoping that their son would be the next rescuer of Israel and lead them to freedom from the Romans. We do not know anything else about this man beyond what Paul says here: he is circumcised (along with Mark and Aristarchus) (**Jews**; "ones of the circumcision" [NRSV]). These three are Paul's only Jewish **co-workers for the kingdom of God** at this point in his ministry; as such, **they have proved a comfort to** Paul (v. 11). Because the kingdom of God movement started as a Jewish movement, I often think about how deeply disappointed many early Jewish followers of Jesus must have been by the lack of continued Jewish involvement on a major scale. Soon gentile followers of Jesus far outnumbered Jewish ones, and Paul himself reflects on this reality in Rom. 9–11. However, this also makes the presence of Jewish coworkers deeply comforting for Paul, as they function as reminders of who God's people are and where they started.

We have similar situations today, as parents are deeply comforted by the child who serves the Lord even if other siblings have wandered away. Leaders in the church are deeply comforted by those faithful members who have stayed and served even through seasons of hardship. Teachers are deeply comforted by students who have been profoundly impacted by their learning and live faithfully because of it, especially when those students share their learning with others. This may also be a reminder for us to thank those people in our lives who taught, mentored, parented, or pastored us. Perhaps we can be a great comfort to them as we remind them that our faithfulness now is due at least partly to their faithfulness.

Our friend **Epaphras** is mentioned next. We already encountered him in Col. 1, where Paul and Timothy note that the Colossian church learned the good news through Epaphras (1:7; see also Philem. 23). Epaphras is a local Colossian man and is greeting his hometown friends (Col. 4:14; compare Onesimus, who is "one of you" [v. 9]). Epaphras is a slave (*doulos* [see comments at 1:7; 4:7]) of Christ, a clear compliment. He demonstrates his slavery by doing what good slaves do: serving his master, Christ. He does so here by **wrestling in prayer** for the Colossians, and the goal of the prayer is that the Colossian Christians will continue to **stand firm in all the will of God, mature and fully assured** (4:12).

Here again Paul (and Timothy) use language for other Christians that he has used of himself. In chapter 1 he tells the Colossians that he and Timothy have been *praying* for them constantly, and with a similar goal in mind: "Since the day we heard about you, we have not stopped praying for you. We continually ask God to fill you with the knowledge of his will through all the wisdom and understanding that the Spirit gives, so that you may live a life worthy of the Lord and please him in every way: bearing fruit in every good work, growing in the knowledge of God" (1:9–10 [see comments there; on prayer, see also 1:3; 4:2–3]). Here it is clear that knowledge of God's will is given through the Spirit; this is what the Colossians always need so that they can become mature and their lives may be "worthy of the Lord and please him in every way" (1:10). This is what we need.

Epaphras is described similarly here, as **always wrestling in prayer** for them. Epaphras also shares Paul's (and Timothy's) purpose: that they **may stand firm in all the will of God, mature and fully assured** (4:12). Paul uses the same verb for "wrestle" or "strenuously contend" in Col. 1:29: "To this end I strenuously contend [*agōnizomai*] with all the energy Christ so powerfully works in me" (also in 1 Cor. 9:25; 1 Tim. 4:10; 6:12; 2 Tim. 4:7). What I find encouraging is that Epaphras seems to find the prayer difficult, just as Paul faces difficulties but perseveres. In other words, it is challenging for Epaphras to pray in this way for his hometown followers of Jesus. Even though he so deeply cares for them and

Laodicea

desires their firmness, maturity, and assurance, the prayer struggle is real. Any of us who have struggled to persevere in prayer know how true this is.

Paul also *testifies to* or *vouches for* what Epaphras has been doing: **working hard for you and for those at Laodicea and Hierapolis** (4:13; see also v. 15; Laodicea is mentioned in 2:1), two neighboring cities (see also Rev. 3:14–22). Does this mean that the Colossians are doubting Epaphras's track record or wondering what he has been doing? Could it be that some Colossians think that the local boy should have stayed home and served? Here Paul assures them that Epaphras is indeed working on their behalf as well as for other Christians in the nearby towns of Laodicea and Hierapolis; **he is always wrestling in prayer** (4:12); **he is working hard** (v. 13).

After Epaphras, two more of Paul's coworkers send greetings to the Colossian church: **our dear friend Luke, the doctor, and Demas** (4:14). Both of these men are known from other letters; in Philemon they are described as fellow workers with Paul (Philem. 24), but in 2 Timothy only Luke remains, for Demas has left Paul: "Demas, because he loved this world, has deserted me and has gone to Thessalonica. Crescens has gone to Galatia, and Titus to Dalmatia. Only Luke is with me. Get Mark and bring him with you, because he is helpful to me in my ministry. I sent Tychicus to Ephesus" (2 Tim. 4:10–12). Notice also that Mark and Tychicus appear in these verses, as they do in Col. 4:7–10. The tradition of the church is that this Luke is the one who wrote Luke's Gospel and the book

Hierapolis

of Acts. As a coworker of Paul, he would have had eyewitness testimony for much of what occurs in the second half of Acts (see the "we" passages in Acts 16:10–17; 20:5–21:18; 27:1–28:16, which indicate that the author is present in those situations).[3]

Luke remains faithful to the end; Demas, however, does not. The situation is in some ways similar to that of Mark, who also deserted Paul (see Acts 15:38), although apparently he reconciled later, as he appears in some of Paul's letters. For Demas we hear of no such resolution. Perhaps he truly loved the world too much (for what it can mean to "love the world," see 1 John 2:15–17).[4] Perhaps this is also why even here in Col. 4:14 Demas is not described as "beloved" or a "fellow slave" or anything similar; he only sends greetings (though he is a "fellow worker" in Philem. 24). Perhaps even at this stage his commitment to Jesus and the image-renewing project is waning, and Paul senses it. Honestly, I find this text and the possible implications to be a cautionary tale. How is it that one could be a coworker of Paul, Timothy, Luke, and Mark—could serve and love and testify with them—and still leave? How could a love of the world overcome all of the beauty and hope that Demas had experienced? Perhaps Demas decided that the cost was too high; following Jesus was not worth it, or at least following Jesus alongside Paul was not worth it. Perhaps he wanted an easier path. There were those who knew Jesus in person and made the same choice (see John 6:66), and even today there are many who do the same.

3. For more detail on the "we" passages, see Keener, *Acts*, 3:2350–74.
4. The tradition about Demas (which is decidedly negative) develops in the second-century AD apocryphal text Acts of Paul (3:1, 4, 12–14, 16).

Paul next asks of the Colossians, **Give my greetings to the brothers and sisters at Laodicea** (4:15). In Laodicea are **Nympha and the church in her house** (v. 15). She is hosting a local church on her property, as did others, including Priscilla and Aquila in Rome (Rom. 16:3–5; 1 Cor. 16:19). In the first century AD churches did not use "church buildings" as meeting spaces; they gathered in homes, in shops, in courtyards, and in gardens. Of course, what is noteworthy here is that the one specific individual who is greeted in Laodicea is a woman. The church is in Nympha's house. We do not know anything else about Nympha, though we do know a great deal about women generally in the ancient Mediterranean world. In that context men held much of the power inside and outside the home (such as in government), but the ancient sources describe many women who were exceptions to this reality. Most women married, but some from elite families did not need to do so; such women had their own houses. This could be true also if the woman had been married but her husband died; wealthy widows did not always remarry. Nympha could have been one of those women, a wealthy woman who committed to the Jesus-movement and was able to offer her home (perhaps a villa with a courtyard) to her local community of Christians. We know from Colossians as well as the Gospels and Paul's other letters that women were consistent and active participants in church life and ministry (see Col. 3:16 and the discussion of that text above).

It is powerful to contemplate how the mention of Nympha here links back to an earlier verse in the letter: "Here there is no Gentile or Jew, circumcised or uncircumcised, barbarian, Scythian, slave or free, but Christ is all, and is in all" (3:11). We have similar language in the famous related text in Galatians: "There is neither Jew nor Gentile, neither slave nor free, nor is there male and female, for you are all one in Christ Jesus" (3:28). All of the people mentioned at the end of the Letter to the Colossians demonstrate "the breadth of the family of believers, for they were Jew (Jesus, called Justus) or Greek (Tychicus); slave (Onesimus) or free (Archippus); male (Luke) and female (Nympha)."[5] The people mentioned here function as an embodiment of the earlier teaching and together are a powerful witness to truth.

There are at least two other meaningful factors here regarding Nympha. The first is a text-critical issue. Some ancient copies of Colossians have the male name "Nymphas" rather than the female name "Nympha." However, the earliest (oldest) manuscript of Colossians (Codex Vaticanus), along with other copies, has the female name. It is easy to see why some in the ancient Mediterranean world would have been uncomfortable with the idea of a woman hosting a church in her house and because of that would have changed her name to a man's name. It is

5. Lewis, "Colossians," 387.

much more difficult to imagine a scenario where there was a male name changed to a female name by several others who were copying Colossians. Jesus led the way in including women in various ways in his ministry, but it was not typical practice in the ancient world; there were people who were uncomfortable with it.

The second factor worth discussing is what it would have cost Nympha to follow Jesus. As a wealthier person with more resources, what would it mean for

---

BIBLICAL BACKGROUND

Women in the New Testament Church

Women appear across the New Testament. We don't have to create them; they are already there. First, women are involved in the ministry of Jesus from the earliest days, as Luke's Gospel makes clear. Luke tells us that the "women were helping to support" Jesus's larger ministry "out of their own means" (Luke 8:3). Women are present at the crucifixion (Matt. 27:55–56; Mark 15:40–41; Luke 23:49; John 19:25–27), and they also are the first witnesses to the resurrection of Jesus (Matt. 28:1–10; Mark 16:1–8; Luke 24:1–12; John 20:1–18). They are present at Pentecost, as the "all" in Acts 2:1 includes the women from Acts 1:14–15. In Luke 10:38–42 the story of Mary and Martha indicates that Mary is training to be a teacher, as her posture at Jesus's feet is one that students took. In Acts 9:2 women are treated as equal participants as targets of Saul's murderous threats; in Acts 16:13–15 Paul and Silas (and Luke, and perhaps others) preach to Lydia and other women, and they baptize her and members of her household; and in Acts 17:4, 12 certain women are described as being prominent.

Women are prophets (Acts 21:9; 1 Cor. 11:5). They are coworkers; Priscilla/Prisca, Euodia, and Syntyche are all described by Paul in this way (Rom. 16:3; Phil. 4:2–3). Priscilla and her husband, Aquila, teach Apollos (Acts 18:2, 26). Phoebe is a deacon or minister (Rom. 16:1; the word *diakonos* can be translated both ways [see discussion at Col. 1:7, 23, 25; 4:7]). Paul also calls Phoebe his "benefactor" and asks the Roman church to receive her (Rom. 16:2). This indicates that she is bringing the letter and would be the first to explain it to the Roman church, functioning as a teacher. Finally, Junia is an apostle (Rom. 16:7). There are some ancient copies of the book of Romans that use a man's name, "Junius," but the best and most reliable copies make clear that she is a woman. (See also the comments on the woman Apphia at Philem. 2.)

her to pick up her cross (Luke 9:23)? What would she need to sacrifice, beyond opening her home, simply because she was able to do so? Jesus teaches often on the dangers of wealth (for example, Luke 6:25; 12:13–21; 18:18–30), and Paul includes greed in his vice lists, labeling it "idolatry" (for example, Col. 3:5). How did these earliest followers of Jesus follow Jesus in the way they used their money, and what can we learn from them? What does following Jesus mean in regard to the money we spend on our housing? On transportation? On clothing? On activities? On food? Is it okay for us to buy an expensive vehicle, a vehicle that is a status symbol, if we can? Or is that a poor use of our resources? When was the last time we purchased something that we did not need? If our relationship to money is never neutral, then we need to keep asking ourselves these questions. We need to ensure that our relationship to money is not selfish but is aligned with God's priorities. God does not value status or status symbols, after all.

We learn more about the relationship between the church in Colossae and the church in Laodicea in the next verse. Paul instructs to them, **After this letter has been read to you, see that it is also read in the church of the Laodiceans and that you in turn read the letter from Laodicea** (4:16). We do not have this letter to the Laodiceans; perhaps someday it will be discovered in an archaeological site. However, we still learn from this text that not only did these two churches know each other, but also they (should have) shared letters so they could learn from the specifics of what was written to each church. This tells us something valuable about the dynamics of the early church, as the goal was for Christians not to live in isolation but to be in ongoing relationship and communication. As we know, isolation can be dangerous in a variety of ways, including the way it often leads to false teaching that is uncorrected simply because there are no other Christians present who can ask good questions and point out weaknesses. As followers of Jesus, we are to have not only non-Christian friends and coworkers (4:5–6) but friends from other churches as well. How many do we have?

Letters in the ancient world were most often read aloud, not silently, at least partly because the majority of people could not read (or write). Picture yourself as a member of the church in Colossae. It is Sunday, the first day of the week (see Acts 20:7), and we have gathered as a church to share our gifts and teach and warn one another (Col. 3:16). We have received a letter from Paul (and Timothy), and now you get up to read the letter aloud to the rest of us (see, for example, 1 Tim. 4:13). There are no chapter and verse markers, so the content itself guides the way you read it. You pause at the appropriate places. You speak dramatically when the content calls for it, and you speak softly and slowly when that tone and pace are best. The rest of us are on the edge of our seats, waiting for the next sentence. Paul and Timothy are largely pleased with us; we have been careful in our discipleship, though Paul does warn us about false teaching (Col. 2:4, 8, 16–23). We have questions, and we turn to Tychicus and Onesimus so that they can help us understand. They have just come from Paul, and part of their role is to answer our questions and guide our understanding. We cannot wait to share this letter with our neighboring church in the next town over! They will have even more questions, but we are well prepared to answer them. We will have someone make a copy so that we can share this letter with them. We will have someone read this letter to us again and again, until we know the content well. We will internalize it, both as individuals and as a community. Some of the vision or instructions will speak to me more powerfully than to you, but other aspects will move or convict you more deeply. We will remind ourselves as a community not to keep wearing our old selves, because our new selves, which are being renewed in the image of our Creator, call us to embody a new life (2:6–4:1).

Before Paul signs off, he gives one final instruction *to the church*; the instruction, however, is for one *specific person* in their community: **Tell Archippus: "See to it that you complete the ministry you have received in the Lord"** (4:17; compare 2 Tim. 4:5). The church *as a group* is to challenge and encourage Archippus in this way. We also hear of Archippus in the Letter to Philemon, where he is called a "fellow soldier" and mentioned alongside the woman Apphia (Philem. 2). We do not know what Archippus's **ministry** (*diakonia* [see comments on *diakonos* at Col. 1:7, 23, 25; 4:7]) is, but clearly he does. The entire church likely knows as well (at least some clearly do—how else would Paul have heard about it?), but even if they do not yet, they will soon, as they are to challenge Archippus to complete it. His *diakonia* is **in the Lord**, which means that ultimately it is from God. It could be a temporary responsibility (such as meeting a need or "slaving" in a specific way) or a more permanent function (perhaps organizing and maintaining a ministry for the church or connecting his own work or trade to the church community or in an evangelistic manner to outsiders), but whatever it is, it is important enough for Archippus's own discipleship and for its impact on others that the entire church is now involved. I wonder: Was he afraid to complete it? Tired? Frustrated? Lazy? If this seems inappropriate to us because we think that this situation should have been handled privately—between Archippus and Paul alone—rather than publicly in a letter, it might be helpful to ponder how some of us have been shaped not by communal contexts but by individualistic ones. Is it really true that our lives should be mostly private? If we are created to be in relationship not just with God but also with others, how much of our lives should involve others, including others who speak into our situations and challenge us? Do we allow this? Do we even have people who know us well enough and whom we trust enough to allow them to challenge us in this way? Colossians 3:16 does insist that Christians teach and warn one another, after all.

The Letter to the Colossians concludes with this verse: **I, Paul, write this greeting in my own hand. Remember my chains. Grace be with you** (4:18). The fact that Paul is writing the greeting at the end in his own hand reminds us that he did not write each word of the letter; Timothy likely did, as the scribe.[6] When Paul asks them to remember his chains, he is asking for their ongoing remembrance, not just a onetime thought (see also Heb. 13:3). In the Bible "remembering" is connected not just to the mind but also to action. For example, when Israel asks God to remember them, Israel is asking God to act on their behalf, not simply to think about them. The same is true at the Last Supper, when Jesus teaches his disciples to continue eating the meal "in remembrance of me" (Luke 22:19; 1 Cor. 11:24). Thinking may be part of it, but the larger point is actually to eat in a way that is connected not only to that one meal but also to the many meals that Jesus ate with people during his life (which crossed social classes and groups and included women). In other words, Paul's request to remember his chains will involve the way that they live and at the very least includes his hope that they keep praying for him (see Col. 4:3–4). It may also include financial support for him (and those in need in their community) or function as a request to allow Epaphras to stay with Paul rather than return home (4:12–13; see also 1:7–8).

Paul's final statement is **Grace be with all of you** (4:18 AT). The "you" is plural in Greek, so he is talking to the entire church. His hope of grace for them is typical of Paul; he makes similar comments elsewhere (1 Tim. 6:21; 2 Tim. 4:22; Titus 3:15; see also Heb. 13:25). For Paul, grace is always caught up in what God has done in and through Jesus (see comments at Col. 1:2, 6; 3:16; 4:6). His hope here is that grace will be present with them, surround them, and shape the way that they live (as the rest of the letter makes clear). His hope would be the same for us. May we live as God created us to live, in the new life available in Christ, as participants in God's image-renewing project, through the power of the Spirit.

6. Compare Rom. 16:22; 1 Cor. 16:21–24; Gal. 6:11–18; 2 Thess. 3:17–18; Philem. 19–25.

Philemon

Greeting Philemon
and the Church

The Letter to Philemon is one of the most underutilized letters among Paul's collection. Its twenty-five verses can seem confusing and even obscure to those of us who live in the twenty-first century. Who is Philemon, after all? Paul's typical style is to write to local churches, not one person, though of course there are the letters to Timothy and Titus as well. The Letter to Philemon is often called a Prison Letter because of Paul's mention of his imprisonment (Philem. 1, 9, 23); it is grouped with the three other Prison Letters: Ephesians, Philippians, and Colossians (see the introduction for comments on Paul's imprisonment and the relationship between the Letters to the Colossians and to Philemon).

This letter is perhaps Paul's most subversive, as Paul resists a key aspect of his own culture: slavery (see extended comments on slavery in the introduction). We see this resistance being channeled through the close friendship that Paul has cultivated with Philemon, his brother in Christ. Get ready for a wild ride, friends. The big question for us is how Jesus might push us to resist key aspects of our own cultures and contexts. In other words, how might following Jesus cost us dearly, both financially and socially, as we walk in discipleship behind Paul, Philemon, and Jesus himself, who paid the highest cost of all?

It is noteworthy that Timothy is mentioned alongside Paul in the opening. The letter begins in good ancient Mediterranean fashion by noting both their *identities* and Paul's *current circumstances*: **Paul, a prisoner of Christ Jesus, and Timothy our brother** (v. 1). Paul's identity is embedded in Christ Jesus, as he belongs to and is a slave of the true Messiah ("Messiah" is from the Hebrew and "Christ" from the Greek, but both refer to the same identity); it is Jesus who determines who Paul is and how he lives and serves. But his current circumstances are difficult; he is in prison, and his imprisonment is because of his allegiance to Jesus (see also vv. 9, 23). As a prisoner, Paul is in a dangerous and marginalized position. Notably, the slave Onesimus is also in a dangerous and marginalized position (including the real threat of imprisonment), so Paul is exhibiting a kind of solidarity with Onesimus here.

Timothy is with Paul (probably as an allowed visitor, not as a coprisoner) as a brother in Christ, a coworker, and probably is the scribe or secretary of this letter.[1] As noted in Col. 1:1 (see extended comments there), Paul is not a solo minister but rather a man deeply committed to community and teamwork; here Timothy is the coworker mentioned. If even Paul needed a team that could hold him accountable and support him appropriately, then we all do as well.

The (first) recipient of the letter is Philemon. He is described as **our dear friend and fellow worker** (v. 1). Notice how Paul does not mention his role as apostle here. He is writing to a **dear friend**, and he will appeal to his friendship with Philemon as the main basis for his request (though he also mentions his imprisonment). Other dear friends of Paul in his letters include local church communities (for example, Phil. 2:12) and individuals, both men and women

---

1. Timothy is mentioned also in Acts 16:1; 17:14–15; 18:5; 19:22; 20:4; Rom. 16:21; 1 Cor. 4:17; 16:10; 2 Cor. 1:1, 19; Phil. 1:1; 2:19; Col. 1:1; 1 Thess. 1:1; 3:2, 6; 2 Thess. 1:1; 1 Tim. 1:2, 18; 6:20; 2 Tim. 1:2; Heb. 13:23.

APPLICATION

Unjust Imprisonment and the Christian Life

Scholar Mitzi Smith connects Paul's imprisonment to that of Martin Luther King Jr., who was also unjustly held in captivity: "Although he is imprisoned under the authority of the Roman Empire, whose appointed officers are his wardens, Paul rhetorically attributes his confinement to Jesus Christ (vv. 1, 9). Oppressed persons can exercise some power or agency over/in their circumstances by, for example, resisting, (re)naming, subverting. . . . While Martin Luther King Jr. languished in a Birmingham jail, he wrote a *Letter from a Birmingham Jail*, answering his critics and insisting on the interconnectedness of all humanity."[a]

a. Smith, "Philemon," 605.

(for example, in Romans, Epenetus in 16:5; Persis in 16:12). The question for us is how we appeal to our close friends in areas of discipleship. How do we walk with them, urging them as beloved ones to live in ways that honor Christ?

Philemon is also a *synergos*, a **fellow worker** (v. 1). Again, Paul has many fellow workers, both men and women. Paul uses the same word, *synergos*, for Priscilla and Aquila in Rom. 16:3; Urbanus in Rom. 16:9; Timothy in Rom. 16:21; Titus in 2 Cor. 8:23; Epaphroditus in Phil. 2:25; Euodia and Syntyche along with Clement in Phil. 4:2–3; Aristarchus, Mark, and Jesus/Justus in Col. 4:10–11; and Mark, Aristarchus, Demas, and Luke in Philem. 24.[2] When I reflect on the contributions of these coworkers, I always think that I would be so honored to be named a coworker by Paul!

Philemon may be the first recipient, but he is not the last. The letter is also addressed **to Apphia our sister and Archippus our fellow soldier—and to the church that meets in your home** (v. 2). We know nothing about Apphia except what Paul tells us here: she is a sister in Christ.[3] She may be Philemon's wife, or she may play some kind of leadership role in the church that meets in Philemon's house. It is women like Apphia who need to be noticed today. There are women in all kinds of roles in the New Testament. We do not have to invent them; they are present,[4] and their service to the kingdom of God and Christ's image-renewing project matters (Col. 3:10; see the sidebar "Women in the New Testament Church" and the comments on Nympha specifically at Col. 4:15).

Likewise, we know very little about Archippus. He appears in Colossians as well. There Paul instructs the entire church to tell Archippus to "complete the ministry [he has] received in the Lord" (Col. 4:17). This is one of many connections between these two letters, one to the Colossians as a whole church and the other to Philemon, Apphia, Archippus, and then (again) the entire church. Archippus may be part of Philemon's household—perhaps his son—or he may simply play some kind of leadership role in the church. He is **our fellow soldier** (v. 2; this word, *systratiōtēs*, is used also of Epaphroditus in Phil. 2:25). This probably means that, along with Paul and Timothy, he is a soldier for Jesus and his kingdom. This is one of many instances of warfare imagery in the Bible. God's people are soldiers and are to fight against their true enemy, Satan (for example, Eph. 6:10–17). There are some Christians today who are uncomfortable with this language, largely due to the effects of colonialism. Some (mostly

---

2. See also 2 Cor. 1:24 (of the church in Corinth).

3. A few ancient manuscripts describe Apphia as "beloved" rather than a "sister," but the majority of copies use the latter word.

4. While some women are named, such as Apphia, other women are included in the more general "brothers and sisters" of the church. We need to imagine many women, including enslaved women, as part of this latter group.

European and American) Christians over the centuries viewed themselves as God's army and then literally conquered people to force conversion. The legacy of misunderstanding the warfare imagery and directing it toward people rather than Satan has created terrible injustices.

Finally, the letter is addressed also to the church that meets in the home of Philemon (v. 2). This early church, like all those in the New Testament (and up through at least the second century AD), met not in a church building but in what we might call nonsacred spaces, such as homes and workshops. The people (not a building) were the church. In continuity with the Old Testament, they were the gathering of God's elect people. The Septuagint, the Greek translation of the Old Testament, uses the word *ekklēsia* to describe Israel when they are gathered in an assembly, and Paul uses *ekklēsia* here of the Colossian Christians. The point is clear: now, in a post-Jesus reality, the Colossians are truly God's people.

Philemon is hosting a house church.[5] We have evidence for the hosts of house churches in multiple New Testament texts, including Mary in Jerusalem (Acts 12:12), Lydia in Philippi (Acts 16:15, 40), Jason in Thessalonica (Acts 17:5–6), Priscilla and Aquila in Rome (Rom. 16:3–5) and in Ephesus (1 Cor. 16:19), Gaius in Corinth (Rom. 16:23), and Nympha in Laodicea (Col. 4:15 [see comments there]). Note how many women's names appear in that list: in a total of eight persons (including Philemon, at the top of the paragraph), four are women—one half.

I often reflect on these texts when I hear people talk of "going to church" today, for they almost always mean a building. Could a tiny shift in language also shift the way we view our identity as God's people? What if we do not "go to church" but instead "go *to be with the church* as God's people"? I also think of these texts when I hear people lamenting the lack of women in the Bible. It may be true that there are more men mentioned, but the women are present as well. Hosts of house churches likely played a significant role in the community, and this is true whether they were male or female. In some ways, actually, hosting a house church would be a "natural" cultural role for a woman to fill, as hosts give structure and often provide food. The practice of eating together was central to the early gatherings of Christians (see Acts 2:46; 20:7; also 1 Cor. 11:17–34, which places the Lord's Supper in the context of a meal), and women were in charge of food preparation (as is still true in most contexts today). Might pentecostals and charismatics, we who insist that the Spirit's indwelling and empowerment are for all and must be lived and experienced by all (rather than being simply true theoretically), be well equipped to notice the spaces

---

5. There were likely several house churches in Colossae, with Philemon hosting just one of them.

in our own cultures where women can lead, whether in culturally typical or surprising ways?

The greeting is next, and as in Paul's other letters, he does not simply say "hello" or "greetings." Instead, we read, **Grace and peace *to you all* from God our father and the Lord Jesus Messiah** (v. 3 AT; compare Rom. 1:7). For Paul, grace and peace are connected to what God has accomplished in and through Jesus (see comments on the scope at Col. 1:2). This greeting is addressed not simply to Philemon but to "you all" or "all of you," as the Greek is plural (see also Philem. 22, 25). Paul and Timothy are well aware of the larger audience for this letter, including how much grace and peace will be needed for Philemon to respond well. Even if Philemon responds as Paul desires, the church community as a whole will need to be able to extend grace and peace to one another as they live toward God's purposes together. The letter is, in that sense, a call to discipleship that all of them need to ponder.

I sometimes wonder about how aware we are of our larger audiences, and if something as simple as our greeting is shaped by our identity in Christ. More specifically, how should we begin interactions with other Christians, either individually or in groups? Do we acknowledge differences (for example, in denomination, culture, gender, class, ethnicity)? Or do we stress what we have in common because we are brothers and sisters in Christ? Or does it depend on the situation? How can we honor Christ well in these moments?

Thanksgiving to God and Praise for Philemon

The thanksgiving section is next, as is typical of letters in ancient Mediterranean culture, and here Paul speaks only for himself and to Philemon (the "you" is singular in Greek): **I always thank my God as I remember you in my prayers** (v. 4; for contrasting examples, see Rom. 1:8–10; Col. 1:3). This indicates that Paul ("I") is the one who is close friends with Philemon ("you"). Philemon is, in that sense, the primary audience. Paul tells Philemon two things: he remembers him in prayer, and he always thanks God for him. The point is regular prayer and regular thanks. Prayer, for Paul, is a key way that Christians embody faith, just as "remembering" in the Bible is not just passive or cerebral but active and embodied (see comments on Col. 4:18). Praying not only for ourselves but also on behalf of others is also significant because it is one way that followers of Jesus serve one another in mutuality (see extended comments at Col. 1:3, 9; 4:2–4, 12). Prayer is a commitment and can often feel difficult, but it is important.

Paul is thankful for Philemon for a specific reason: **because I continue to hear of your love and faithfulness, which you have for the Lord Jesus and for all the holy ones** (v. 5 AT; more references to love occur in vv. 7, 9).[1] Philemon's reputation is solid; he loves **Jesus** well, and he loves the **holy ones** (*hagios*) well. **Love** in the Bible is always connected to commitment and sacrifice; love in the Bible is not (just) feelings but is lived. It also has a "goal" (*telos*) in that it

---

1. A survey of various English translations of verses 5–6 shows differences among scholars regarding how best to translate them (and thus understand the nuances). For discussion, see Thompson, *Colossians and Philemon*, 212–16.

is redemptive. In other words, the common cultural view of love as feelings or tolerance is not the biblical view of love, which directs us always toward living in the Spirit, living toward *God's purposes* (not our own), and becoming more like Christ.

Philemon's love for the "holy ones" is reminiscent of what Paul says to the entire church in the Letter to the Colossians (see comments at Col. 1:2, 4, 12, 22, 26; 3:12). This fits well with Philemon's **faithfulness** (*pistis*). Faithfulness is also about lifestyle. Here some English versions use the word "faith" to translate the Greek word *pistis*, which can be translated in a variety of ways, including "faith, faithfulness, trust." Even if we use the word "faith," we know that real faith affects our actions. If we say that we have faith in our marriages or friendships, we will live in ways that show that to be true. The same is true for our faith in Jesus, as pentecostals and charismatics have often emphasized. We must live our faith, which is why altar calls and ongoing repentance and growth in holiness are key in our contexts. It is also true that we have seen some major moral failings in recent years, with some well-known leaders and communities publicly exposed as not truly living the faith they profess. Texts such as Philem. 5 convict and remind us to practice what we preach, both individually and in community.

After stating why he is thankful for Philemon (v. 5), Paul gives the content of his prayers for Philemon, which includes the idea that Philemon will live the truth of what he says he believes, an action that will in turn circle back to affect his belief: **I pray that your *partnership* with us in the faith may be effective in deepening your understanding of every *good thing* we share for the sake of Christ** (v. 6). This prayer is connected to a **good thing** (*agathos*) that Paul will soon ask Philemon to do regarding Onesimus, a slave. Paul specifies that favor later (also using *agathos* [v. 14]), telling Philemon what **partnership** (*koinōnia*) means (see *koinōnos* in v. 17), but here Paul simply lays the foundation. In other words, Philemon's partnership is to be one of active participation—generosity, even—that will shape the way he thinks. Actions have a way of doing that, of course. If we do something that we know is good and right and God-honoring, even if we do not feel like doing it, we often say afterward, "Well, that was good for me. I'm glad I did it. *Doing* it affected me in a way that just *thinking* about it would not have. Actually, doing it has shaped the way I think about it." I am on the prayer team at our church, but sometimes I do not feel like participating in the partnership of prayer. My husband can build and fix almost anything, and his help is often requested by people in our church, but especially in busy seasons he can feel reluctant. However, when we pray and fix *despite* our feelings, afterward we are almost always glad to have participated. The simple act of doing these things shapes the way that we think about them.

Regarding partnership, it's important to note that elsewhere in Paul's letters he links the ideas of partnership/sharing and the Spirit explicitly (for example, 2 Cor. 13:14; Phil. 2:1). Here in Philemon Paul prays that Philemon's understanding may be deepened (v. 6), and the Spirit is the one who gives understanding (connected to wisdom and knowledge) in Colossians (compare Col. 1:9; 3:10, 16 and comments there).

Before transitioning to the body of the letter, Paul makes one more statement of thanksgiving: **Your love has given me great joy and encouragement, because you, brother, have refreshed the hearts of the Lord's people** (v. 7). Philemon's love has already refreshed the **hearts** or (metaphorical) "entrails" (*splanchnon*; also in vv. 12, 20 [see comments at Col. 3:12]) of others among the **Lord's people**, his "holy ones" (*hagios*; also v. 5 [see comments at Col. 1:2, 4, 12, 22, 26; 3:12]). Soon Paul will ask for that refreshment once again when his request regarding Onesimus is made clear (v. 20; compare Rom. 15:32; 1 Cor. 16:18); Paul will be refreshed if Philemon welcomes Onesimus as a brother, not a slave (vv. 16–17). And to top it off, Paul calls Philemon **brother**, not "friend." In other words, the power of family is at work here—not biological family but Jesus-family. And Paul wants Philemon to act accordingly, to grow even more in his discipleship and maturity. If we sense here a kind of "buttering up," we are correct. Paul is indeed preparing Philemon for what he will ask more directly later in the letter, but this is not manipulative. It was expected for the thanksgiving sections of ancient letters to contain this kind of content; if Paul had not included it, his audience would have been surprised at his breach of etiquette and wondered why he was upset.[2] In other words, if we think that such comments are inappropriate, we should consider how we have been shaped by contexts that are different than Paul's context and attempt again to understand Paul's world.

Paul's attention to the way in which he communicates is noteworthy here; he carefully lays the foundation for what he needs to say. How many of us are so careful in our own relationships and are attentive to our audience in this way, especially when it concerns another person's or group's discipleship? How might we encourage someone else to take the next step in their walk with Jesus? Here Paul first praises Philemon for his love and partnership before asking him to extend that partnership. This is a powerful lesson for all of us.

---

2. Compare Galatians, which moves from the greeting to the body of the letter without including the thanksgiving. The reason is clear: Paul was unhappy with them.

PHILEMON 8-22

Paul's Appeal for Onesimus

Paul transitions next to the request itself, as the **therefore** in verse 8 indicates. "Therefore" means "for this reason," and it is for the reason already given—Philemon's faithful love and partnership (vv. 5–7)—that Paul proceeds to ask what he does regarding the slave Onesimus, which is that Philemon receive him as a brother (v. 16). This is what Philemon **ought to do** (v. 8). The Greek word here is *anēkō*, which can also be translated as "fitting." In Col. 3:18 Paul uses it in the household code in regard to the wives who submit as is "fitting" in the Lord (the only other appearance of *anēkō* in the New Testament is in Eph. 5:4). What is fitting here in the Letter to Philemon is how Philemon should receive Onesimus as a brother, not as a slave (v. 16). In other words, what is fitting is a completely countercultural reception and treatment of Onesimus, which suggests that what is "fitting" in Col. 3:18 is countercultural as well, a redefinition of submission that does not simply copy the way the world sees submission but instead transforms it in Christ (see comments at Col. 3:18).

Such countercultural embodiment raises the question of how well we as Christians today resist the cultural defaults of the contexts where we live. Do we have the kind of discernment that allows us to see what must be resisted culturally because of our allegiance to Jesus and his kingdom rather than the kingdoms of this world? This may apply economically, politically, socially, in entertainment, in sexuality, or in other areas. Because the challenge in the Letter to Philemon is primarily social and economic (as Onesimus is a slave whose labor is owned economically and whose low status is managed by social stratification), the more specific question for us is whether we resist the economic and social realities that take advantage of others and treat them as lesser. How can the church create and foster a new reality, a kingdom-of-God reality, where "there is no Gentile or Jew, circumcised or uncircumcised, barbarian, Scythian, slave or free, but Christ is all, and is in all" (Col. 3:11)?

Paul admits, **Although in Christ I could be bold and order you to do what you ought to do, yet I prefer to appeal to you on the basis of love** (vv. 8–9). Philemon has led with love in the past (v. 5), and Paul asks him to continue to do so here. As we know, if we have to order someone, even if it is appropriate in Christ to do so with boldness, we have not addressed the heart issue. Anyone can follow an order, which can also encourage them not to take responsibility for whatever action they take (since it was not their idea). Persuading someone, getting them to buy into the idea, is a bigger win. The Holy Spirit indwells and empowers us; by practicing dependency on the Spirit, we should be the most persuasive people on the planet!

Paul reminds Philemon of his chains and his age, calling himself **an old man and now also a prisoner of Christ Jesus** (v. 9). Elders are greatly respected in cultures that prioritize the community over the individual, as in the ancient Mediterranean world, and imprisonment would be especially challenging for an older man (see also vv. 1, 23, and the introduction for comments on Paul's chains and the Prison Letters). In other words, Paul has earned the right to speak; his life has been one of consistent commitment and sacrifice. Have we earned the right to speak into difficult situations because of our consistent commitment and sacrifice?

Paul then specifically appeals to Philemon on behalf of Onesimus (see all Col. 4:9), saying that he **became** his **son while** he **was in chains** (v. 10). In other words, Onesimus is not Paul's biological son but his spiritual son (compare 1 Thess. 2:11).[1] How often in the ancient Mediterranean world do you think people used family language like "son" for slaves? Not often. Paul here is redefining his relationship with Onesimus, who is Philemon's slave (v. 16), in a way that challenges and encourages Philemon to do the same. Because of the ancient Mediterranean culture's focus on honoring the elderly there is added pressure here, as children were expected to care for aging parents. Onesimus is thus the one who as "son" needs to assist his "father," "the imprisoned and vulnerable apostle."[2]

The name "Onesimus" means "useful" or "beneficial" and was a common name for both free and enslaved men in the Roman Empire (compare the language of "benefit" in v. 20). This is helpful background information because next Paul uses a play on words: **Formerly he was useless to you, but now he**

---

1. Paul can also use maternal, rather than paternal, imagery for himself. See 1 Cor. 3:1–2; Gal. 4:19; 1 Thess. 2:7.
2. Batten, "Philemon," 245.

has become useful both to you and to me (v. 11). Onesimus has been "useless" to Philemon because he is no longer with him (perhaps also because of misuse of resources, if that is the case [see v. 18]). Now, however, Onesimus is "useful," at least partly because he has become a Christian.[3]

It is helpful to clarify here what Paul is asking in verses 10–12. His appeal regarding Onesimus seems to include a careful request that after Paul sends Onesimus back to Philemon, Philemon should then allow Onesimus to *return to Paul*. Because Onesimus has been so useful to Paul, Paul wishes for Onesimus to continue that service. Paul argues that Onesimus has now become useful to Philemon as well (v. 11). This could refer to Onesimus's contribution to Philemon's household or perhaps even to the church that meets in Philemon's home (v. 2). It could also more specifically be communicating that Onesimus, if returned to Paul, could then function with Paul as a kind of agent for Philemon.[4]

Paul is bold here, but not in commanding Philemon. He is bold in stressing that Onesimus is useful to him and to Philemon, which is a challenge to Philemon. How will he interact with Onesimus going forward? How do we interact with people, especially those who have been unhelpful or devalued or marginalized in the past (perhaps even by us), in order to live out a new reality with Jesus at the center of it? What does love require of us, if love's goal is always redemptive and moves us closer to Christ?

Philemon's opportunity is near, as Paul is sending Onesimus back to Philemon (v. 12). The question is what Philemon will do when Onesimus arrives. Paul stresses his deep appreciation for Onesimus again; Onesimus is not only his (spiritual) son but Paul's **very heart** (*splanchnon*), his (metaphorical) "entrails" (v. 12; also in vv. 7, 20 [see comments at Col. 3:12]). We might say that Paul is laying it on pretty thick. But for what purpose? In order to get something for himself? No. Paul is attempting to get something for Onesimus, a slave. If Onesimus is a runaway slave, Paul knows that by returning Onesimus to his master, Onesimus could face all kinds of brutal punishments, including beatings. Paul does not want that to happen. He knows, however, that culturally and legally, a slave owner has the power to treat slaves in this way. Paul wants Philemon's loyalty to Christ to affect how he treats his slave here, and Paul is working hard to persuade him in this positive direction. If Onesimus did not run away but was sent by Philemon or with Philemon's permission (see the introduction for discussion of the options), then Onesimus's position is less precarious—though of course Philemon, as owner, still has legal control over Onesimus and what happens to him. The question for us is how often we lay it on pretty thick for

---

3. Eric Barreto comments that Onesimus's "worth . . . is not based on his utility but on the kinship these followers of Jesus now share" ("Philemon," 616).
4. Dunn, *Epistles*, 329.

selfish reasons rather than for the sake of others. We want our spouse to assent to a purchase of clothing, activities, or household goods. We want a close friend to assent to our idea or activity. We want a boss to promote us. We want a teacher to give us the good grade. When was the last time you laid it on thick on behalf of someone else, someone who could not return the favor? This totally one-sided approach should remind us of Jesus, who used his life for the sake of others (see especially Phil. 2:6–11).

Paul adds, **I would have liked to keep him with me so that he could take your place in helping me while I am in chains for the gospel** (v. 13; see also vv. 1, 9–10, 23). Paul wishes to keep Onesimus (the slave) so that he can take the place of Philemon (the master) in helping Paul. That is how useful Onesimus is; he can take Philemon's place at Paul's side. Think about this from Philemon's perspective. As a slave owner, his culture has reinforced for him the idea that he is superior to slaves. That is simply the cultural norm. But now Paul is resisting that norm and placing Onesimus and Philemon on the same level. How might Philemon have felt about Onesimus being on his same level? Would he have been surprised, or angry, or frustrated, at least at first? But then, after that initial feeling had passed, would he have been able to ponder the truth of what Paul is saying in Christ, where there is no slave or free (see Col. 3:11)? What are the ways in which our cultures and contexts reinforce notions of who is superior and who is inferior? Does it have to do with money? Fame? Power? Skin color? Beauty? Intelligence? Creativity?

Paul stresses again that he is *not commanding* Philemon; he is *persuading* him. He wants Philemon to make the decision himself: **But I did not want to do anything without your consent, so that any favor you do would not seem forced but would be voluntary** (v. 14; compare 2 Cor. 9:7; 1 Pet. 5:2). The **favor** here is *agathos* in Greek, a "good thing." Paul employs this term earlier in the letter, in the thanksgiving section (v. 6), when he is laying the foundation for his request to Philemon. Paul is requesting, and he wants Philemon to consent voluntarily, to choose for himself with full understanding of what his choice means.

Finally, more than halfway through the letter, Paul states clearly and explicitly what he would like Philemon to do: welcome Onesimus **no longer as a slave, but better than a slave, as a dear brother** (v. 16). Paul adds that **perhaps** (*tacha*) there is a *divine reason* for what has happened between Onesimus and Philemon, a reason that led to their separation (v. 15; *tacha* was often used to convey divine direction): it is so that they could come back together as brothers in Christ (v. 16) after Onesimus became a Christian. There is a parallel in the Old Testament in the story of Joseph's brothers, who sold him into slavery. Later, in Egypt, Joseph tells them that there is a divine reason behind it all, as "God intended it for good" (Gen. 50:20).

Masters are the clear social and legal superiors to slaves, but brothers are social peers—equals. In this letter first Timothy is a "brother" (*adelphos* [v. 1]), then Philemon is a "brother" (*adelphos* [v. 7]), and now Onesimus is a **dear brother** (*adelphos agapētos* [v. 16; compare Matt. 23:8; Acts 1:16]). Onesimus is also described as a "dear brother" in the Letter to the Colossians (*agapētos adelphos* [Col. 4:9]; the word "dear" [*agapētos*] is used of Philemon in Philem. 1). Being brothers in Christ means that there is a deep, long-term commitment, as members of healthy families live in ways that honor and support one another through all the ups and downs of life. Our siblings in Christ will still be our siblings in Christ when God's image-renewing project is complete and new creation is fully here, so this relationship really is eternal. Are we living the truth of it now? Are we living toward our future?

There is a contrast here between how dear Onesimus is to Paul (very!) and how dear he is or should be to Philemon (even dearer!) (v. 16). Whether or not Philemon actually agrees at this point does not matter, as Paul is attempting to persuade Philemon that it is the truth. If Philemon receives his slave not as a slave but as a brother, how will that benefit him? Might Onesimus be very dear to him, **both as a fellow man and as a brother in the Lord** (v. 16)? The word for **Lord** here is *kyrios*, which can also be translated "Master" (see discussion at Col. 3:22–4:1); Jesus, of course, is our true Master (see also 1 Cor. 7:22). In other words, Paul is reminding Philemon subtly (or not so subtly?) that Jesus is our Master, which places Philemon and Onesimus on the same level as slaves of Jesus. They are also brothers in the Master, another clear point that they are on the same level.

Many have asked if the phrase **no longer as a slave** (v. 16) means that Paul is asking Philemon to free Onesimus. In other words, is Paul asking Philemon simply to treat his slave better, perhaps even only when the church is gathered in Philemon's house (and there is an audience),[5] or is he asking him to release Onesimus? The act of releasing a slave is called manumission, and it was relatively common in the Roman Empire, though apparently it was viewed with suspicion by some.[6] Slaves sometimes could purchase their freedom; slaves could also be granted freedom by their masters for their faithful service. However, manumitted slaves typically were permanently obligated to render certain services to their former masters, so there were still strings attached.

Over the centuries many scholars have argued for the former—Philemon should treat his slave better—at least partly because of what Paul says about

---

5. Lloyd Lewis mentions this possibility ("Philemon," 442).
6. Marianne Meye Thompson notes, "It was suspected that corrupt and unclean persons were too frequently set free. Augustus therefore set minimum age limits both for those who wanted to manumit slaves and for the slaves themselves" (*Colossians and Philemon*, 221).

slavery in the household codes in texts such as Col. 3:22–4:1. However, a growing number of scholars today see in this language (along with Paul's larger argument) a request to Philemon to free his slave.[7] This is due to the fact that in this letter Paul is writing to a dear friend, not to a church that includes some people who do not know him well. Paul can push a friend harder, in the context of intimate relationship, than he can push acquaintances or strangers. Even here Paul does not say "Free your slave" directly, but many scholars have noted that such direct language does not necessarily make sense culturally (as Paul's world simply assumed the presence of slavery) and could actually have resulted in Paul losing his audience. In other words, Philemon might have stopped listening. Paul's language is careful, but if Philemon actually takes Paul's wishes seriously and ponders what that might mean for his life, he will end up realizing that he needs to free Onesimus. But he will come to that conclusion on his own, without feeling forced. Such an act certainly would cost Philemon socially. Many others in his socioeconomic class or status would likely abuse him verbally and perhaps avoid him socially and economically (hurting his trade or business) because of his resistance of the status quo. His honor is at stake here, and in an honor-shame context, honor is the highest goal in life.[8] The question for us is whether we ever resist the status quo in our contexts because of our loyalty to Jesus and commitment to participation in the kingdom of God.

Paul really pulls out all the stops in the final verses of the letter: **So if you consider me a partner, welcome him as you would welcome me. If he has done you any wrong or owes you anything, charge it to me. I, Paul, am writing this with my own hand. I will pay it back—not to mention that you owe me your very self** (vv. 17–19). Philemon obviously does consider Paul to be a **partner** (koinōnos). Paul has already used "partnership" language earlier in the letter (koinōnia [v. 6]). Their partnership means that Philemon should welcome Onesimus as he would welcome Paul—as a partner. They are not only brothers; they are partners, another peer-based category that stresses mutual participation and identity.

Paul also knows that there has been tension between Onesimus and Philemon, and Paul attempts to defuse it by taking responsibility for paying back anything that is owed (v. 18; compare Col. 3:13). This could be hypothetical, as Paul says **if he has done you any wrong or owes you anything,** but it is more

---

7. For example, McCaulley, *Reading While Black*, 152–57.

8. Bruce Wintle and Bruce Nicholls add another point of tension: "If Philemon gave Onesimus his freedom too quickly, simply because he had become a Christian and was living a new life, other Christian slaves in the church would also demand their freedom. Besides, other slaves would perhaps make a show of becoming Christians in order to obtain their freedom" (*Colossians and Philemon*, 197).

likely that Paul is speaking tactfully because he knows there has been a problem. The **wrong** could have been the financial debt or the debt could have followed from the wrong. In other words, if the wrong is Onesimus running away (if Onesimus is in fact a runaway slave), then the debt could be missed work. Or the wrong could be the debt and indicate that Onesimus is guilty of theft, either in terms of missed work or poor work (if Onesimus is a manager of Philemon's estate or business, perhaps), or even the stealing of the fare to travel to where he met Paul. If Onesimus is a debt slave, then missing work is an offense, and Paul is offering to pay the debt. After full payment of the debt, Onesimus would then be a freedman. There are clear parallels here to the way that Jesus pays our debts for us (see also the "debt" language in Matt. 18:21–35).

In verse 19 Paul adds that he is writing this himself (compare, as examples, 1 Cor. 16:21; Gal. 6:11; Col. 4:18). In other words, Paul is not using a scribe for this part of the letter (or perhaps even for the entire letter), even though that is the typical practice in his culture. He is serious enough to write it himself. He is also serious about the next statement, written personally, where he reminds Philemon that Philemon owes Paul his **very self** (v. 19). I always chuckle when I read this last line, because Paul adds the comment in a way that almost feels like an afterthought, though it is not. Have you ever been talking with your spouse or friend or sibling and added something like, "I won't even mention what happened at lunch last time!" Of course, even making that statement makes a statement; it brings to mind exactly what happened at lunch last time, which is obvious because both of you know it. This reminder to Philemon that Philemon owes Paul his **very self** is probably the sharpest piece of Paul's attempt to persuade Philemon, and appropriately, he saves it for near the end. Leading with this kind of statement will not get us very far in winning people over, as most of us know. Building an argument in ways that are powerfully persuasive tends to work much better.

What does Paul mean when he says that Philemon owes Paul his **very self**? It seems to be connected to why Philemon is even a Christian. In other words, Paul is (not so) gently reminding Philemon that Philemon is part of the Jesus-community, the image-renewing, kingdom-of-God reality, only because of Paul.[9] Paul is the reason for Philemon's new "self." He says, in effect, "If 'debts' are under review, you owe infinitely more to me than Onesimus does to you! I have not 'charged' you, my son in the faith; you should not 'charge' Onesimus, who is now your Christian brother. But if you choose to, I will pay on his behalf."[10]

---

9. Philemon lives in Colossae, and the Letter to the Colossians makes clear that Paul did not help to plant the church there; Epaphras did (Col. 1:7–8; 4:12; also mentioned in Philem. 23). However, Philemon could have been converted through Paul's witness in a variety of other locations, including Ephesus, a neighboring city.

10. Harris, *Colossians and Philemon*, 238.

This language of owing one's "very self" to someone else may seem to be an overstatement, and perhaps even inappropriate, unless we are talking about owing ourselves to Jesus. In individualized contexts we tend to think of ourselves as self-made and self-identified, but in collective contexts people make sense of themselves by their connection to family and community. In other words, in Paul's context it makes sense to remind Philemon of their relationship, as it has deeply formed Philemon in his "very self." I am a mother and a professor, and I have invested deeply in many people in terms of their Christian formation, including my kids and some of my students. Saying that someone owes me their "very self" may even be true in a sense if I led them to Christ. It is not an exaggeration to say that I expect a return on that investment; not to me, but I do want them to pay it forward in their participation in the kingdom of God. To whom do you owe your "very self" in this way?

And now Paul wants Philemon to live that truth. It is one thing for Philemon to have heard Paul teach that there is no slave or free in Christ (for example, Gal. 3:28; Col. 3:11); it is quite another for Philemon to live the reality of it. Living the truth of the gospel will cost someone like Philemon more than it will cost others, simply because he has more to lose. This is true in so many areas of our lives, including money, status, independence/individuality, and power. What if we took another's debts/obligations because we could, even if it would be difficult? Even if it would mean that we would lose money, status, independence, or power? What if we did this because other followers of Jesus needed it, because they were contributing to the kingdom of God in other ways? Think of someone whom you consider a social peer, or even better, think of someone you actually consider to be a bit higher than yourself. Now think about someone you consider socially below you. Perhaps it is the person who lives in a trailer park or on the street, the person who cannot afford to eat organic food or in restaurants, the person who does not have your academic or creative ability. Now imagine that person as your sibling, your brother or sister, your partner.

After reminding Philemon about his own debt (to Paul), Paul calls Philemon his **brother** again (v. 20). He stresses his wish: **That I may have some benefit from you in the Lord** (v. 20; recall that the name "Onesimus" means "useful" or "beneficial" [see comments at v. 11]). Paul commented earlier that Philemon had "refreshed the hearts of the Lord's people" (v. 7); now Paul asks for Philemon to refresh Paul's heart, his innermost being or (metaphorical) "entrails" (*splanchnon* [v. 20]; see also vv. 7, 12, and comments at Col. 3:12).

Paul adds another layer of pressure in the next verse, stressing his confidence in Philemon: **Confident of your obedience, I write to you, knowing that you will do even more than I ask** (v. 21). The obedience is much more to the gospel and Jesus as Lord/Master than to Paul, of course.[11] This is what it means for Philemon to follow Jesus in his time and place. What does it mean for us to follow Jesus in our times and places? What must we sacrifice on behalf of other Christians, even if our broader non-Christian culture tells us we do not need to do so?[12]

Paul actually says that he knows Philemon will do even more than what he asks (v. 21). Is the "more" something specific or not? It could be manumission, which means releasing Onesimus from slavery. However, manumitted slaves were permanently obligated to render certain services to their former master. Could the "more" here be a release even from those obligations?

Now, near the end of the letter, Paul adds that he hopes to visit: **And one thing more: Prepare a guest room for me, because I hope to be restored to you in answer to your prayers** (v. 22; compare 2 Cor. 1:11; Phil. 1:19; 2:24; Col. 4:3–4). The "you" and "your" in this verse are plural in Greek (for the first time since v. 3), so here Paul is addressing the entire church that meets in Philemon's house. Paul's impending visit also provides motivation for Philemon to do what Paul asks, of course. If and when Paul arrives, will Philemon have been faithful in his response? Will Philemon's commitment to Jesus have revolutionized the way that he interacts with Onesimus, as a brother rather than a slave (v. 16)? And how will the larger church have responded to the situation?

---

11. R. González, "Philemon," 310.

12. In 2 Corinthians Paul asks the Corinthians to sacrifice financial resources to support Jewish followers of Jesus in Judea who are in danger of literally starving to death. For language that parallels the Letter to Philemon, see 2 Cor. 8:8; 9:4, 13.

Final Greetings and Blessing

At the conclusion of the letter Paul mentions that Epaphras sends greetings to Philemon (v. 23 [the "you" is singular in Greek]). Epaphras is a local Colossian man who helped to plant the church there (see Col. 1:7–8; 4:12–13 and comments there); he is also Paul's coworker and **fellow prisoner in Christ Jesus** (v. 23; see also v. 1; compare Rom. 16:7; Col. 4:10). The implication is that Epaphras knows what Paul is asking Philemon to do. This is also true for the others who greet Philemon, including Mark, Aristarchus, Demas, and Luke (v. 24). All four of these men appear in the Letter to the Colossians, as does Onesimus (Col. 4:9–10, 14 [see discussion there]). They are Paul's fellow workers (v. 24), as is Philemon (v. 1), and they know what the situation is. In other words, because Paul includes other people in the letter, this situation is public, not private. It is not just a quiet discussion between two friends; Paul makes sure that other Christians know what Paul is asking Philemon to do.

Paul ends the letter by addressing the community as a whole: **The grace of the Lord Jesus Messiah be with the spirit of you all** (v. 25 AT).[1] Paul often mentions grace, which in his letters is connected to Jesus, the Messiah/Christ and Lord/Master (for example, Philem. 3; see Col. 1:2; 4:18 and comments there). The "you" is plural here again, indicating one spirit for all of them. In this way Paul addresses the communal spirit of Philemon and the entire assembly (also in Gal. 6:18; Phil. 4:23), persons who, together, have a spirit that is open to the Spirit of God.[2] Do we think of ourselves today as having a communal spirit,

---

1. The earliest and most trusted copies of this letter do not include an "amen" at the end or any subscriptions (that include, for example, another mention of Philemon or Rome as the location).

2. See Dunn, *Epistles*, 349.

or are we too focused on our individual spirits? What could it look like for us to embrace this and communally share a spirit that is open to the Holy Spirit? And how might God use one person or group to challenge another person or group in their Spirit-empowered discipleship, in ways that prompt them to live *toward* rather than *against* God's purposes, even/especially when it might have economic and social costs?

Many modern readers think that Paul should have pressured Philemon (and other slaveholders) much harder. In this view, the injustice of slavery is so terrible, and so obvious, that Paul should have done more to combat it, perhaps even calling for the abolition of the entire system. The question here is what it means for us to take Paul seriously as a person of his own time. In his context, where no one had called for the abolition of slavery, can we appreciate Paul's careful but insistent push for justice in a letter like Philemon?

Other modern readers have disliked Paul's direct pressure on Philemon. They see Paul as pushing too hard, and perhaps even being manipulative. Their view is that Paul should allow Philemon to make his own choices, on the basis of his own conscience; the situation is between him and God alone. First of all, if that is our response, then we should consider how we have been shaped by individualized contexts that tell us that everything is or should be private. Many collectivist contexts (like Paul's), even today, do not view life as mostly private. Also, Paul and Philemon clearly are good friends; they know each other well. The question for us is how hard we can and do push in our closest friendships and relationships when something connected to the kingdom of God is on the line. I hope that we all have people who can push us well and even make us uncomfortable in healthy ways in our discipleship. This is especially important in places where the dominant culture tells us that we are not only allowed to but in fact should live into our "true selves," whatever and whoever they may be. However, when a fellow brother or sister in Christ decides that they can follow Jesus on their own terms, disregarding what the Bible and centuries of Christian tradition have to say about greed or inappropriate language or sexual immorality (see comments at Col. 3:5–11), we must respond to it. It is our responsibility, and even more so if the person is a friend. Challenging conversations, steeped in prayer, are the first step.

Finally, Paul is spending his social capital, but not for himself. He is doing so on behalf of someone else, someone without that social capital. He is spending it on behalf of a slave, someone considered property in that context. When was the last time we spent social capital on behalf of someone who did not have any (or had very little), someone who could not repay us for our sacrifice? When was the last time we offered our energy, finances, reputations, and time in service of those whom Jesus values but are not valued (at least in the same way) by the world? What has following Jesus cost us, especially economically and socially (as it would have cost Philemon)?

When I imagine my way into the situation with Paul, Philemon, Onesimus, and the church, I imagine Paul thinking, "I don't really want to do this. God, please send someone else. I don't want to risk my relationship with Philemon, who is a good friend of mine. I also don't want to risk jeopardizing his support for the church in Colossae. There is so much at stake here, but the most important thing is Onesimus. He's a new Christian and friend of mine, and he needs someone to advocate for him. I can do it, so I should do it. And Philemon can change. Anyone can change with the Spirit's help—look at me, after all." Then I imagine Philemon's response: "Paul, how dare you! You're worrying me here with what you're asking me to sacrifice. But part of the reason I joined the Jesus-community is the way it treats people. You have been saying for years that there is no slave or free in Jesus" (Col. 3:11). Then the church that gathers in Philemon's house, which includes Apphia and Archippus (Philem. 2), thinks, "Wow, Paul! This is a big ask. What will Philemon do? And what will we do, as a community, in response to your request?" Finally, I imagine Onesimus thinking conflicting thoughts: "I can't believe that Paul is doing this for me! I'm shocked in some ways but not in other ways. Paul is a radical, and his vision of God's kingdom is so powerful. But I'm a bit fearful of Philemon and how he'll respond. He has all the legal and cultural influence. Can he ever truly see me as a brother? How will I respond to him if he doesn't? Perhaps even more importantly, how will I respond to him if he does?"[3]

How will we respond, friends? What might love—a commitment that involves sacrifice and points toward God's purposes—require of us in our own contexts, our own cities and countries and centuries? Where is the Spirit leading us? And what will it cost us?

---

3. Matthew Johnson, James Noel, and Demetrius Williams argue that Onesimus "has been mentioned, discussed, referenced; subtly present, but voiceless, powerless, hidden in the shadows and without agency" (*Onesimus Our Brother*, 1). Through my historically shaped imagination I am attempting to exhibit his voice and presence.

Bibliography

Balabanski, Victoria S. *Colossians: An Eco-Stoic Reading*. Earth Bible Commentary. London: T&T Clark, 2020.

Barclay, John M. G. "The Gift Perspective on Paul." In *Perspectives on Paul: Five Views*, edited by Scot McKnight and B. J. Oropeza, 219–36. Grand Rapids: Baker Academic, 2020.

Barreto, Eric D. "Philemon." In *The Letters and Legacy of Paul*, edited by Margaret Aymer, Cynthia Briggs Kittredge, and David A. Sánchez, 613–20. Fortress Commentary on the Bible. Minneapolis: Fortress, 2014.

Barth, Markus, and Helmut Blanke. *Colossians: A New Translation with Introduction and Commentary*. Translated by Astrid B. Beck. Anchor Bible 34B. New York: Doubleday, 1994.

Batten, Alicia J. "Philemon." In *Philippians, Colossians, Philemon*, edited by Mary Ann Beavis, 201–64. Wisdom Commentary 51. Collegeville, MN: Liturgical Press, 2017.

Beale, G. K. *Colossians and Philemon*. Baker Exegetical Commentary on the New Testament. Grand Rapids: Baker Academic, 2019.

Bowens, Lisa M. *African American Readings of Paul: Reception, Resistance, and Transformation*. Grand Rapids: Eerdmans, 2020.

Bruce, F. F. *The Epistles to the Colossians, to Philemon, and to the Ephesians*. New International Commentary on the New Testament. Grand Rapids: Eerdmans, 1984.

Cadwallader, Alan H. "Colossae." Bible Odyssey. Accessed July 9, 2024. https://www.bibleodyssey.org/articles/colossae/.

Callahan, Allen Dwight. "Letter to Philemon." In *A Postcolonial Commentary on the New Testament Writings*, edited by Fernando F. Segovia and R. S. Sugirtharajah, 329–37. The Bible and Postcolonialism. London: T&T Clark, 2009.

———. "Paul's Epistle to Philemon: Toward an Alternative *Argumentum*." *Harvard Theological Review* 86 (1993): 357–76.

Calvin, John. *The Epistles of Paul the Apostle to the Galatians, Ephesians, Philippians and Colossians*. Translated by T. H. L. Parker. Grand Rapids: Eerdmans, 1965.

Colkmire, Lance. "Bow or Burn." *Church of God Evangel*, January/February 2021, 12–13.

Danker, Frederick W., ed. *A Greek-English Lexicon of the New Testament and Other Early Christian Literature*. 3rd ed. Chicago: University of Chicago Press, 2000.

Davids, Peter H. "Colossians." In vol. 16 of *Cornerstone Biblical Commentary*, edited by Philip W. Comfort, 227–312. Carol Stream, IL: Tyndale, 2008.

———. "Philemon." In vol. 16 of *Cornerstone Biblical Commentary*, edited by Philip W. Comfort, 415–37. Carol Stream, IL: Tyndale, 2008.

Dunn, James D. G. *The Epistles to the Colossians and to Philemon: A Commentary on the Greek Text*. New International Greek Testament Commentary. Grand Rapids: Eerdmans, 1996.

Fee, Gordon D. *God's Empowering Presence: The Holy Spirit in the Letters of Paul*. Peabody, MA: Hendrickson, 1994.

Fitzmyer, Joseph A. *The Letter to Philemon: A New Translation with Introduction and Commentary*. Anchor Yale Bible 34C. New Haven: Yale University Press, 2008.

Foster, Paul. *Colossians*. Black's New Testament Commentaries. London: Bloomsbury T&T Clark, 2016.

Garland, David E. *Colossians and Philemon*. NIV Application Commentary. Grand Rapids: Zondervan, 1998.

González, Awilda. "Colossians: Paul's Teaching and Its Implications for the Latinx Church." In *Latinx Perspectives on the New Testament*, edited by Osvaldo D. Vena and Leticia A. Guardiola-Sáenz, 241–52. Lanham, MD: Lexington Books / Fortress Academic, 2022.

González, Rudolph D. "Philemon: A 'Useful' Letter *para el Pueblo de Dios*." In *Latinx Perspectives on the New Testament*, edited by Osvaldo D. Vena and Leticia A. Guardiola-Sáenz, 307–17. Lanham, MD: Lexington Books / Fortress Academic, 2022.

Green, Joel B. *The Gospel of Luke*. New International Commentary on the New Testament. Grand Rapids: Eerdmans, 1997.

Gupta, Nijay K. *Colossians*. Smyth & Helwys Bible Commentary. Macon, GA: Smyth & Helwys, 2013.

Guyon, Jeanne de la Mothe. *Jeanne Guyon's Christian Worldview: Her Biblical Commentaries on Galatians, Ephesians, and Colossians with Explanations and Reflections on the Interior Life*. Translated by Nancy Carol James. Eugene, OR: Pickwick, 2017.

Hamm, Dennis. *Philippians, Colossians, Philemon*. Catholic Commentary on Sacred Scripture. Grand Rapids: Baker Academic, 2013.

Harris, Murray J. *Colossians and Philemon*. Exegetical Guide to the Greek New Testament. Nashville: B&H Academic, 2010.

Hnin, Thawng Ceu. "The Letter to Philemon." In *An Asian Introduction to the New Testament*, edited by Johnson Thomaskutty, 405–21. Minneapolis: Fortress, 2022.

Horgan, Maurya P. "The Letter to the Colossians." In *The New Jerome Biblical Commentary*, edited by Raymond E. Brown, Joseph A. Fitzmyer, and Roland E. Murphy, 876–82. Englewood Cliffs, NJ: Prentice-Hall, 1990.

Ireland, Bill, and Dock Hollingsworth. *Philippians & Philemon, Colossians*. Preaching the Word. Macon, GA: Smyth & Helwys, 2018.

Johnson, E. Elizabeth. "Colossians." In *Women's Bible Commentary*, edited by Carol A. Newsom, Sharon H. Ringe, and Jacqueline E. Lapsley, 585–87. 3rd ed. Louisville: Westminster John Knox, 2012.

Johnson, Matthew V., James A. Noel, and Demetrius K. Williams, eds. *Onesimus Our Brother: Reading Religion, Race, and Culture in Philemon*. Minneapolis: Fortress, 2012.

Keener, Craig S. *Acts: An Exegetical Commentary*. 4 vols. Grand Rapids: Baker Academic, 2012–15.

———. *The IVP Bible Background Commentary: New Testament*. 2nd ed. Downers Grove, IL: InterVarsity, 2014.

———. *The Mind of the Spirit: Paul's Approach to Transformed Thinking*. Grand Rapids: Baker Academic, 2016.

———. "Mutual Submission Frames the Household Codes." Paper presented to the Biblical Studies Interest Group at the 50th Anniversary Meeting of the Society for Pentecostal Studies, Southlake, TX, March 19, 2021.

———. *Paul, Women and Wives: Marriage and Women's Ministry in the Letters of Paul*. Peabody, MA: Hendrickson, 1992.

Keener, Craig S., and Glenn Usry. *Defending Black Faith: Answers to Tough Questions about African-American Christianity*. Downers Grove, IL: InterVarsity, 1997.

Keesmaat, Sylvia C. "Colossians." In *The Letters and Legacy of Paul*, edited by Margaret Aymer, Cynthia Briggs Kittredge, and David A. Sánchez, 557–72. Fortress Commentary on the Bible. Minneapolis: Fortress, 2014.

Knox, John. *Philemon among the Letters of Paul: A New View of Its Place and Importance*. Rev. ed. New York: Abingdon, 1959.

Lewis, Lloyd A. "An African American Appraisal of the Philemon-Paul-Onesimus Triangle." In *Stony the Road We Trod: African American Biblical Interpretation*, edited by Cain Hope Felder, 233–46. Minneapolis: Fortress, 1991.

———. "Colossians." In *True to Our Native Land: An African American New Testament Commentary*, edited by Brian K. Blount, 380–88. Minneapolis: Fortress, 2007.

———. "Philemon." In *True to Our Native Land: An African American New Testament Commentary*, edited by Brian K. Blount, 437–43. Minneapolis: Fortress, 2007.

Lohse, Eduard. *Colossians and Philemon: A Commentary on the Epistles to the Colossians and to Philemon*. Translated by William R. Poehlmann and Robert J. Karris. Edited by Helmut Koester. Hermeneia. Philadelphia: Fortress, 1971.

Lutz, Cora E. "Musonius Rufus, the Roman Socrates." *Yale Classical Studies* 10 (1947): 3–147.

Lyons, George, Robert W. Smith, and Kara Lyons-Pardue. *Ephesians, Colossians, Philemon: A Commentary in the Wesleyan Tradition.* New Beacon Bible Commentary. Boston: Beacon Hill, 2019.

Lyons, Michael A., and Jacob Stromberg, eds. *Isaiah's Servants in Early Judaism and Christianity: The Isaian Servant and the Exegetical Formation of Community Identity.* Wissenschaftliche Untersuchungen zum Neuen Testament 2/554. Tübingen: Mohr Siebeck, 2021.

MacDonald, Margaret Y. "Can Nympha Rule This House? The Rhetoric of Domesticity in Colossians." In *Rhetoric and Reality in Early Christianities*, edited by Willi Braun, 99–120. Waterloo: Wilfrid Laurier University Press, 2005.

———. *Colossians and Ephesians.* Sacra Pagina 17. Collegeville, MN: Liturgical Press, 2000.

———. *The Power of Children: The Construction of Christian Families in the Greco-Roman World.* Waco: Baylor University Press, 2014.

———. "Slavery, Sexuality and House Churches: A Reassessment of Colossians 3.18–4.1 in Light of New Research on the Roman Family." *New Testament Studies* 53, no. 1 (2007): 94–113.

MaGee, Gregory S. *Portrait of an Apostle: A Case for Paul's Authorship of Colossians and Ephesians.* Eugene, OR: Pickwick, 2013.

Martin, Ralph P. *Ephesians, Colossians, and Philemon.* Interpretation. Atlanta: John Knox, 1991.

McCaulley, Esau. *Reading While Black: African American Biblical Interpretation as an Exercise in Hope.* Downers Grove, IL: IVP Academic, 2020.

McKnight, Scot. *The Letter to Philemon.* New International Commentary on the New Testament. Grand Rapids: Eerdmans, 2017.

———. *The Letter to the Colossians.* New International Commentary on the New Testament. Grand Rapids: Eerdmans, 2018.

Meyer, Joyce. *Battlefield of the Mind: Winning the Battle in Your Mind.* Rev. ed. New York: FaithWords, 2011.

Moo, Douglas J. *The Letters to the Colossians and to Philemon.* Pillar New Testament Commentary. Grand Rapids: Eerdmans, 2008.

Murphy O'Connor, Jerome. "Colossians." In *The Pauline Epistles*, edited by John Muddiman and John Barton, 204–15. Oxford Bible Commentary. Oxford: Oxford University Press, 2010.

Osborne, Grant R. *Colossians & Philemon: Verse by Verse.* Bellingham, WA: Lexham, 2016.

Osiek, Carolyn. *Philippians, Philemon.* Abingdon New Testament Commentary. Nashville: Abingdon, 2000.

Pao, David. *Colossians and Philemon.* Zondervan Exegetical Commentary on the New Testament. Grand Rapids: Zondervan, 2012.

———. "Serving Our Master: Colossians 3:24." In *Devotions on the Greek New Testament: 52 Reflections to Inspire and Instruct*, vol. 2, edited by Paul Norman Jackson, 102–4. Grand Rapids: Zondervan, 2017.

Paschke, Boris. "Four Early Christian Documents from Egypt Regarding Prayer to the Holy Spirit." *Pneuma* 44, no. 1 (2022): 5–19.

Philip, Finny. "The Letter to the Colossians." In *An Asian Introduction to the New Testament*, edited by Johnson Thomaskutty, 311–29. Minneapolis: Fortress, 2022.

Richter, Sandra L. *Stewards of Eden: What Scripture Says about the Environment and Why It Matters*. Downers Grove, IL: InterVarsity, 2020.

Saarinen, Risto. *The Pastoral Epistles with Philemon and Jude*. Brazos Theological Commentary on the Bible. Grand Rapids: Brazos, 2008.

Schweizer, Eduard. *The Letter to the Colossians: A Commentary*. Translated by Andrew Chester. Minneapolis: Augsburg, 1982.

Seitz, Christopher R. "The Book of Isaiah 40–66: Introduction, Commentary, and Reflections." In *The New Interpreter's Bible*, edited by Leander E. Keck, 6:309–552. Nashville: Abingdon, 2001.

———. *Colossians*. Brazos Theological Commentary on the Bible. Grand Rapids: Brazos, 2014.

Smith, Mitzi J. "Philemon." In *Women's Bible Commentary*, edited by Carol A. Newsom, Sharon H. Ringe, and Jacqueline E. Lapsley, 605–7. 3rd ed. Louisville: Westminster John Knox, 2012.

Still, Todd D. "Colossians." In *Ephesians–Philemon*, edited by Tremper Longman III and David E. Garland, 263–360. Expositor's Bible Commentary 12. Rev. ed. Grand Rapids: Zondervan, 2006.

Sumney, Jerry L. *Colossians: A Commentary*. New Testament Library. Louisville: Westminster John Knox, 2008.

Swindoll, Charles R. *Philippians, Colossians, Philemon*. Swindoll's Living Insights New Testament Commentary. Carol Stream, IL: Tyndale, 2017.

Thompson, Marianne Meye. *Colossians and Philemon*. Two Horizons New Testament Commentary. Grand Rapids: Eerdmans, 2005.

Usry, Glenn, and Craig S. Keener. *Black Man's Religion: Can Christianity Be Afrocentric?* Downers Grove, IL: InterVarsity, 1996.

Vasser, Murray. "Grant Slaves Equality: Re-examining the Translation of Colossians 4:1." *Tyndale Bulletin* 68, no. 1 (2017): 59–71.

Wacker, Grant. *Heaven Below: Early Pentecostals and American Culture*. Cambridge, MA: Harvard University Press, 2001.

Wansink, Craig S. "Philemon." In *The Pauline Epistles*, edited by John Muddiman and John Barton, 263–67. Oxford Bible Commentary. Oxford: Oxford University Press, 2010.

Williams, Demetrius K. "'No Longer as a Slave': Reading the Interpretation History of Paul's Epistle to Philemon." In *Onesimus Our Brother: Reading Religion, Race, and*

Culture in Philemon, edited by Matthew V. Johnson, James A. Noel, and Demetrius K. Williams, 11–46. Minneapolis: Fortress, 2012.

Wilson, Robert McL. *A Critical and Exegetical Commentary on Colossians and Philemon*. International Critical Commentary. London: T&T Clark, 2005.

Wintle, Bruce, and Bruce Nicholls. *Colossians and Philemon: A Pastoral and Contextual Commentary*. Asia Bible Commentary. Carlisle, UK: Langham Global Library, 2019.

Witherington, Ben, III. *Conflict and Community in Corinth: A Socio-rhetorical Commentary on 1 and 2 Corinthians*. Grand Rapids: Eerdmans, 1995.

Wright, N. T. *Colossians and Philemon: An Introduction and Commentary*. Tyndale New Testament Commentaries 12. Downers Grove, IL: IVP Academic, 2008.

———. *Scripture and the Authority of God: How to Read the Bible Today*. New York: HarperOne, 2005.

Youssef, Bishop. *Colossians, 1 Thessalonians, 2 Thessalonians*. Orthodox Christian Bible Commentary. Sandia, TX: St. Mary & St. Moses Abbey, 2016.

Zerbe, Gordon, and Muriel Orevillo-Montenegro. "Letter to the Colossians." In *A Postcolonial Commentary on the New Testament Writings*, edited by Fernando F. Segovia and R. S. Sugirtharajah, 294–303. The Bible and Postcolonialism. London: T&T Clark, 2009.

Index of Authors

Index of Scripture
and Other Ancient Sources